TREKKING IN THE ATLAS MOUNTAINS

ABOUT THE AUTHOR

Karl Smith has been a keen walker and climber since his childhood, growing up on the fringes of the Lake District. A former trekking guide, Karl has worked in Greece, the Alps, Nepal and Turkey as well as Morocco. He has written several other guides, including *The Mountains of Turkey* (also published by Cicerone Press).

Karl Smith is currently Senior Lecturer in Tourism at Harper Adams University College, Shropshire, with a particular interest in small-scale tourism and adventure tourism.

He is married with a daughter, Abigail, and still runs walking tours in his spare time – most recently in the Pindos Mountains, Greece, and on the via ferrata around Lake Garda, Italy.

TREKKING IN THE ATLAS MOUNTAINS

by
Karl Smith

2 POLICE SQUARE, MILNTHORPE, CUMBRIA LA7 7PY
www.cicerone.co.uk

© Karl Smith 2004
ISBN 10: 1 85284 421 3
ISBN 13: 978 1 85284 421 9

First edition 1989
Second edition 1998
Third edition 2004, reprinted 2006

Acknowledgements

Space permits me to mention only a few of the many people who have helped me write this book. For those who accompanied me on numerous trips and made my time in Morocco so enjoyable, thanks also.

For the original edition, I would especially like to thank Jan Campbell, Alice England, Alan Keohane, Pam Lucas, Maureen McMurtry, Steve Parker, Mike Wynn (now of Walks Worldwide) and Peter the truck driver (whose surname escapes me).

For this third edition, I am indebted to Jon Crawford, who produced the Jebel Sahro map. Jim Gayler provided me with useful information following his trip to the Toubkal area. Birmingham College of Food and Tourism gave me time to work on the book – a luxury made more welcome when compared to the effort of writing the original guide. Thanks particularly to Sarah Thomas of the Research Department, and to Dave Luke for awarding me this time.

Cover photo: Assaka n'Ait Ouzzine (Jebel Sahro)

CONTENTS

Advice to Readers

Readers are advised that while every effort is taken by the author to ensure the accuracy of this guidebook, changes can occur which may affect the contents. It is advisable to check locally on transport, accommodation, shops, etc. The publisher would welcome notes of any such changes.

Map Key

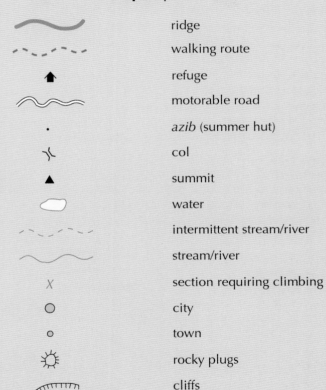	ridge
	walking route
	refuge
	motorable road
	azib (summer hut)
	col
	summit
	water
	intermittent stream/river
	stream/river
X	section requiring climbing
	city
	town
	rocky plugs
	cliffs

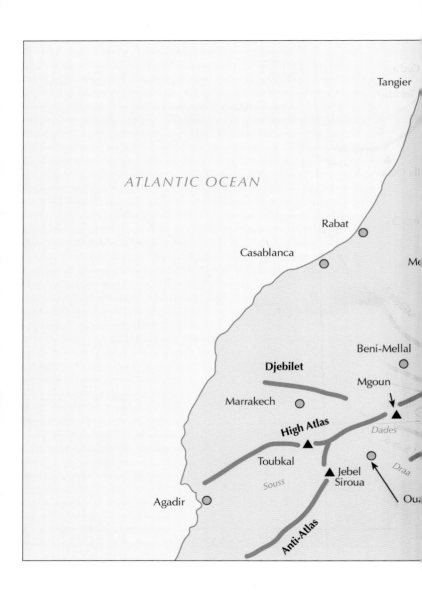

ATLANTIC OCEAN

Tangier

Rabat

Casablanca

Me

Beni-Mellal

Djebilet

Mgoun

Marrakech

High Atlas

Dades

Toubkal

▲ Jebel
Siroua

Souss

Draa

Agadir

Oua

Anti-Atlas

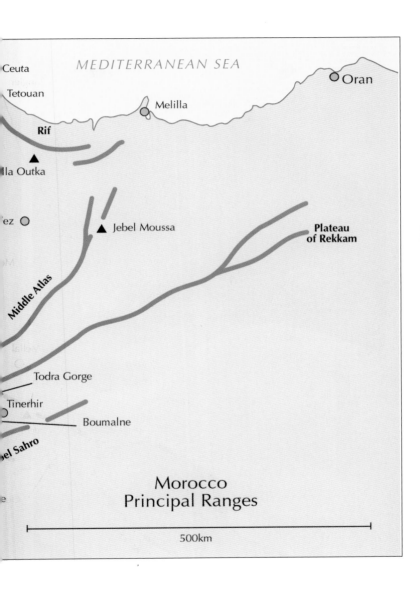

Ceuta

MEDITERRANEAN SEA

Oran

Tetouan

Melilla

Rif

▲
lla Outka

ez ○

▲ Jebel Moussa

**Plateau
of Rekkam**

Middle Atlas

Todra Gorge

Tinerhir

Boumalne

el Sahro

Morocco
Principal Ranges

500km

Threshing wheat, Tissili (Mgoun)

PREFACE TO THE THIRD EDITION

Much has changed for the visitor to Morocco since I researched the original book back in the late 1980s. Fortunately these changes have, by and large, affected only the ease of travel rather than the essential experience. Technological advances mean automated cashpoints in the cities, and internet booking is now the norm. The steady influx of trekkers to the region has led to more facilities, whether these be humble tea-shacks or old kasbahs converted into luxury hotels. The degree of development has reflected the amount of tourism – the ever-popular Toubkal area has consequently seen the biggest changes. Mgoun, Jebel Sahro and Jebel Sirwa are now regular features in numerous adventure travel company brochures, but here the effect on the ground is less evident. By the standards of, say, the Alps or Pyrenees, the Moroccan mountains are still remote and, for the greater part, scarcely touched by tourism. On the tours described you may well encounter other Western trekkers, but you are still going to experience an authentic Moroccan way of life rather than an economy geared towards accommodating tourists' needs.

Keeping a guidebook up to date is a never-ending task – a guest-house opens, while another nearby closes; 20 dirhams for a room becomes 30; the 8 a.m. bus now departs at 7 a.m. I have tried to incorporate significant changes whether these be transport, accommodation or prices. Other areas are more contentious, and chief amongst these is the question of route timings. This has provoked more response in my mailbag than any other aspect of the book. On balance, most of the comments have been to the effect that my timings are on the mean side. In my defence I would say that all the routes in this book were walked (and timed) with groups – usually slower than an individual's walking pace. Additionally, those who use the book and find times generous are unlikely to write in and complain for fear of seeming boastful. I have therefore decided to leave the timings as I originally found them.

The information in this guide is as up to date as possible, but if readers experience something different, I firstly apologise and secondly invite them to contact me with relevant information via the publishers. All information is gratefully received, and useful contributions will be acknowledged in any future edition.

Karl Smith, 2003

Eroded pinnacles on the Taggourt plateau (Jebel Sahro)

INTRODUCTION

For European visitors, traversing the 15 miles or so of the Gibraltar straits affords one of the most dramatic contrasts imaginable. The difference is not merely between the Christian and Islamic world, but a more fundamental contrast between European and African traditions. In short, Morocco and the Atlas mountains is probably the most accessible 'exotic' destination for western Europeans, a fact which ensures its continuing popularity.

Pliny, the great Roman geographer, on seeing the Atlas peaks, described them as 'the most fabulous mountains in all of Africa'. Stretching southwards from the Mediterranean coast in an arc for a thousand miles, they are certainly the highest and most extensive range in North Africa. For the walker and mountaineer they offer an incredible variety of scenery, climate and terrain. Within the valleys one can observe a way of life that has changed little during the last thousand years; the word unique can be used with justification. While the wild scenery may be reminiscent of parts of Central Asia, a closer look at the way of life here dispels any such notion. The native inhabitants of this region, the Berbers, possess a distinctive culture. Their villages of kasbahs, surrounded by steep terraces, are of a special beauty and leave a lasting impression on the visitor.

Exploration of these mountains by Europeans began in earnest with the arrival of French colonists, and their 40-year protectorate means that most summits have been ascended. Nowadays, the area around Jebel Toubkal and its approaches has established itself as a popular destination for walkers from all over Europe. Journey beyond these narrow confines, however, and you are unlikely to meet anyone other than the native Berber inhabitants.

While opportunities for rock-climbing do exist (and there are some very good opportunities), this book is primarily aimed at the walker and scrambler. Whatever your age or level of fitness the Atlas mountains are a rewarding and exciting destination, easily reached from Europe.

This book covers the Toubkal region, which contains the highest and most spectacular peaks, and also describes circuits in the less well-known but equally impressive Mgoun massif area, Jebel Sahro range and Jebel Sirwa. Other areas of interest are described briefly.

Geography

The Atlas mountains form several ranges. The **High (or Grand) Atlas** runs roughly east-north-east from the Atlantic coast near Agadir as far as northern Algeria, where they diminish and curve eastwards, forming the **Saharan Atlas**. In the central High Atlas, another range strikes north-eastward. This is the **Middle Atlas**, the main watershed of the country. At the southern end of the High Atlas, a separate range runs parallel to the south and east. This is the **Anti-Atlas**. Jebel Sahro forms the eastern end of this range, and is separated from both the main Atlas chain and the Anti-Atlas by the Dades valley, which runs into the main Draa valley. Further west, the High Atlas and Anti-Atlas are separated by a broad, fertile valley known as the Souss. The Sirwa area lies between the High Atlas and Anti-Atlas. Finally, there are the Rif mountains, parallel to the Mediterranean coast in the north.

The High Atlas range holds the most interest for the walker, and forms the bulk of this book. West and east of Marrakech two motor roads cross the High Atlas via passes: the Tizi-n'Test to the west and the Tizi-n'Tichka to the east, and they form the boundaries of the **Toubkal Atlas**. Immediately to the east lies the **Central High Atlas**, a large area which extends as far as the Plateau

Approaching the Toubkal Refuge, with the slopes of Toubkal on the left, and Ouanoukrim in the background

des Lacs and Imilchil. This region contains the M'goun massif and the fertile Ait Bougoumez valley.

Beyond the Tizi-n'Test one enters the **Western High Atlas**. This remote area has much to offer the walker. There are many interesting summits over 3000m from Igdat (3616m) to Jbel Tinergwet (3551m).

Geology

The first phase of Atlas development took place during the Carboniferous era, when marine Palaeozoic sediments were affected by severe pressure, resulting in intense folding and mountain building (this Hercynean orogeny was also responsible for much European mountain formation). This land was then eroded to a flat or gently undulating peneplain. The second phase of development resulted in further wearing down and the deposition of sediments. The third phase, beginning in the middle of the Tertiary period, started with renewed folding, resulting in the mountains as we know them today. The folding was accompanied by down-sinking, leading to the formation of basins such as the Souss, and by volcanic eruptions. Jebel Sirwa is an example of the latter. The fourth phase added little to what previously existed. Torrential erosion has thrown thick alluvial deposits over the basins at the foot of the Atlas.

In the Toubkal area the rock consists of volcanic green andesites, rhyolites and tuffs. These are ancient rocks laid bare, forming the area's characteristic jagged peaks and steep-sided valleys. Detritus suggests that small glaciers may have existed in the higher cirques, but otherwise the area was not glaciated (as can be deduced from the numerous spurs which project into the valleys). In places what appears to be moraine is usually debris from landslips. The village of Aroumd is built on such debris, from what must have been an enormous landslip.

The Central High Atlas are characterised by extensive outcrops of fairly soft Permian–Triassic strata. They are simply folded rock structures, with broad open synclines and sharp anticlines (such as Jebel Ghat). In places rivers have cut down through the soft rock to produce deep gorges, another characteristic feature in the Mgoun area. The Jebel Sahro and Anti-Atlas are of a totally different origin and structure. They are part of the great elevated mass of the African plateau, and are formed of old schists and hard quartzites. Additionally, there are substantial masses of overlying conglomerate in the Jebel Sahro area, and this provides the characteristic scenery of spectacular towers and eroded plateaux.

CLIMATE – WHEN TO GO

It is possible to walk and climb in the Atlas throughout the year. Despite the proximity to the Sahara the summer temperatures in the mountains are generally bearable. While it can reach

Springtime, Aroumd

125°F (51°C) at midday in Marrakech, up in the hills it may only be a pleasant 70°F (low 20s °C). Walking in the lower valleys can, however, be rather hot. At night in summer it rarely gets chilly except on the higher peaks.

The best time to visit is probably in late spring. At this time the winter snows have not entirely melted, the visibility is better than in high summer, and daytime temperatures are pleasant. It is warm enough during the day to be in shirt sleeves, although at night a good sleeping bag is needed. In autumn the weather becomes noticeably cooler, and towards the end of September snow showers can be expected on the higher peaks. At this time of year there is abundant ripe fruit in the valleys, a welcome addition to the

diet. Early winter is a time best avoided: cold, often wet and without the benefit of firm snow underfoot. Late winter can give some of the finest days here, with clear skies, when ski-ing and sunbathing are both equally possible. On bad winter days a warm duvet may be useful, as it can get down to -20°C.

Storms can occur at any time of the year, but usually give plenty of warning of their approach. Rain turns to snow on the higher peaks by October. Temperatures on these peaks can be decidedly chilly, even in midsummer if there is any wind about. Toubkal is notorious in this respect, and anyone choosing to bivvy here can expect frost throughout the year.

Here, as elsewhere in the world, weather patterns over the past few years have become erratic and often extreme. Snow has been scarce during winter, with heavy falls in spring and torrential storms in summer. Be aware of the dangers of flash floods – never camp in river beds.

A mention should be made of Ramadan. The timing varies each year, but it is approximately 10 days earlier each year – check a diary to find the exact period. As Muslims fast during daylight hours, you may find it difficult to obtain the services of muleteers, and locals may be more reluctant to provide food during the day.

VEGETATION AND WILDLIFE

One of the most noticeable features of the Atlas is their barrenness, yet despite this there is a wide variety of interesting plants to be seen. Most famous of the trees is, perhaps, the Atlas cedar (*Cedrus atlanticus*). The former extensive forests have gone from the High Atlas, though are still to be found in the Middle Atlas and Rif. Elsewhere the thuya (*Arbor-vitae*), much used in box-making for its patterned wood, is often found on the lower slopes, together with juniper. The endemic argan is found in the far west of the Atlas.

In the limestone areas of the Atlas many familiar herbs are to be found, such as lavender, rosemary and thyme. The dry terraces are covered in thorny scrub, the result of centuries of over-grazing. Many of the flowers are similar, or identical, to those found in the Mediterranean regions. The best time to observe these flowers is in late

Orchid, Jebel Sahro

spring, when the winter snows have just melted. Narcissi and crocuses are followed by squill and asphodel. Kermes oak, arbutus, wormwood, lentisk, myrtle and mastic dominate the lower slopes of the Atlas.

While a comprehensive description of the flora is beyond the scope of this book, those interested should refer to *Catalogue des Plants du Maroc* by E. Jahandiez and R. Negre, or *L'Afrique du Nord* by R. Marie (illustrated).

The Atlas are very sparsely populated with wildlife. Most likely to be encountered is the Barbary ground-squirrel; beyond that you may be fortunate and sight a mouflon, the large-horned sheep. Perhaps the most famous animal is the Barbary ape, which is still found in the Middle Atlas and on the northern slopes of Taska n'Zat. In many places there are still wild boar. Diminishing populations of gazelle, lynx, wildcat and striped hyena also exist. It is possible that leopards also still exist; lions disappeared only in 1922. The pressures on land and resulting deforestation mean that the future for many of the animal species is uncertain.

Snakes and reptiles, including chameleons, are numerous. Snakes are not often encountered in the areas described, and will generally move off at the sound of footfalls. However, they can be sluggish, sunning on rocks or paths, and walkers should be observant. More widespread, but concentrated in certain areas, are scorpions. To miminise the chance of

The fields of Imhilene, the first greenery seen after crossing the Tizi n'Ouanoums

an encounter, clear areas round tents, zip doorways and never reach under stones. While there is no need to be overly fearful about snakes and scorpions, do be aware of the risks. A sting or snakebite far from any hospital could have serious consequences.

The Atlas are home to several endemic species of butterfly, the one most likely to be encountered being the Giant grayling (*Berberia abdelkader*).

Very rewarding for the naturalist is the birdlife: amongst the species endemic to the area are the Barbary partridge, Moussier's redstart and Levaillant's green woodpecker (*P. vaillantii*). In the cities and towns the Common bulbul is both frequent and noisy. Other notable sights include rollers (*Coracias garrulus*), abundant in places such as the Ait Bougoumez valley, while Booted and Bonelli's eagle are not uncommon. The mountains of the High Atlas are the home of the lammergeier (*Gypetus barbatus*) and Egyptian vulture; although not numerous, there is a reasonable chance of seeing both these species in the Toubkal area. Choughs and alpine choughs are common, and on the plains heading towards the hills it is possible to see egrets, sandgrouse and the elusive Great bustard.

The Jebel Sahro region has a noticeably more exotic avian fauna. Several species of sandgrouse occur (though more heard than seen), and the rock towers of the Taggourt plateau are a good place to see the Barbary falcon.

For further information see the bibliography at the end of the book.

HISTORY AND CULTURE – THE BERBERS

Rock carvings found in the Atlas indicate that this area has been inhabited for at least 12,000 years. The first inhabitants were the Berbers, who still constitute a large part of the population of Morocco and are by far the dominant ethnic group in the mountain regions.

The origins of the Berbers are unclear. They are believed by some to be Caucasian in origin, to have crossed the straits of Gibraltar from Europe and to have spread gradually throughout north-west Africa (the Maghreb). Elements in their architecture, still unchanged in the mountains, link them to Pharaonic Egypt. On the other hand, lozenges and chevrons found today on rugs reflect early Asian or southern European designs, as does the pottery.

Very early in their history the Berbers were divided into three major tribes: the Sanhajas, Zenatas and the Masmoudas. Of these the Masmoudas were the ones who settled in the Atlas, Rif and Anti-Atlas as farmers, while the other tribes adopted a nomadic existence.

During the Roman occupation of North Africa, known by them as Mauretania, the Berbers were left

Young local, Jebel Sahro

largely untouched. Originally practising agrarian, animistic religions (some of which may have been adopted by the Romans) they were subsequently 'converted' to Judaism. This was at best a nominal conversion, possibly manufactured by Jews, some of whom (as part of the great dispersion) fled to Morocco after the destruction of the Jerusalem Temple in AD 70. The Jews remained in Morocco through the centuries, forming a small but influential community with its own specific identity.

With the arrival of St Cyprian the Berbers 'converted' to Christianity, although once again this was very loosely practised. It was not until the arrival of Islam that the Berbers found

a religion to which they adhered strictly. Today, the Berbers are almost universally Muslim, of the Shi'ite sect.

Islam came with the Arab invasion of the Maghreb at the end of the seventh century. This produced lasting changes in Morocco, where the Arabs are today, by and large, the ruling race. While the Berbers took to Islam they did not accept Arab rule as readily, nor did they adopt Arabic as their language.

During the years following the Arab invasion, the ever-increasing tide of Islam took Arab and Berber alike into Spain, where they remained until the fall of Granada in 1492. By this stage Morocco had become an isolated, backward-looking country divided into two kingdoms: Fez and Marrakech (the name Morocco is a corruption of 'Marrakech'). So it was to remain for the next few centuries, resisting the influence of Turkey though being invaded variously by Portugal and Spain. Then, towards the latter part of the 19th century, a new influence made itself felt in Morocco; the arrival of the French. By 1912 the country had become a French protectorate. For the next 40 years the French introduced civil reforms, constructed railways and roads, and greatly expanded the economy. This came to an end in 1956 when Morocco was formally granted independence under Mohammed V.

Morocco is now an independent monarchy under Mohammed VI. Much of the country's recent history

has, however, failed to influence the way of life of the Berbers, who have remained isolated from Morocco's economic and social progress.

Architecture

No guide to the Atlas would be complete without a mention of the local architecture. The first sight of a Berber hill village removes any illusion a visitor may have of still being in Europe. The cubic, flat-topped village houses of mud or stone stand out against the steep hillsides and give the Atlas their unique character. In parts of the Atlas, and in the valleys to the south, the famous kasbahs are still to be found. These buildings are of indeterminate age – the Glaouis' fortress, for example, now in decay, is relatively modern, though has every

Ruined Kasbah, Dades valley

appearance of dating back to the Middle Ages. The village houses with their wood drainage-gutters, wooden locks and flat earth roofs reinforce this impression. In a country where transport is difficult it is inevitable that the architecture uses local materials in its construction. The buildings in the Atlas are made of mud, stone and above all *pisé*, the local mud pressed between wooden boards and dried. Most of the kasbahs are constructed of this material.

While in the Toubkal region there are little other than flat-topped, straight-sided village houses, in areas such as the Mgoun massif and Anti-Atlas more characteristic examples of Maghreb architecture are to be found. The buildings of interest can be divided into three sorts: the kasbah, the *ksar* and the *agadir*. The kasbah, the most frequently encountered, is a tall fortified house of square ground-plan, with distinctive tapering walls. These are pierced by narrow slits similar to lancet windows in a medieval castle. The four corners are usually projecting. The *ksar* (plural *ksour*) is more commonly found to the south-east of the High Atlas (for example in Risani, Erfoud), and is more definitely a sort of Roman *castrum*, being oblong and surrounded by an unbroken wall of even height. Usually larger than a kasbah, a *ksar* contains the houses of an extended family or tribe within its perimeter wall. Finally, the *agadirs* are great fortified grain storehouses, of major importance to the villagers. In times of strife they could provide accommodation as well as storage. These can be seen, for example, in the Tessaout or Aït Bougoumez valleys.

The origins of the architecture of the kasbah, which is unique in form, lie in the tribal existence which prevailed here for millennia as the tribes grew from extended families to units of several families. Clearly defensive in function, the kasbah enabled the whole family together with its livestock to shelter inside it in times of intercommunal strife. The watchtowers at each corner of the kasbah served to warn of enemy approach.

Stylistically the origins of this architecture are harder to determine. There are two main areas where it may have originated. Firstly Yemen, the former Arabia Felix, where the present-day buildings are somewhat similar in proportion; and secondly Pharoanic Egypt, where the pyramids, temples and other sloping-walled buildings may, some experts believe, have served as inspiration. It was the Arabs, however, who brought to Morocco the peculiar tapering kasbah tower-shape. The first examples of such structures in the Maghreb are in the minarets of the mosques at Kairouan (AD 670) and at Sfax (9th century). The enclosing walls and patio forming the centre of the kasbah main house are thought to have their origins in the Roman-Byzantine *castellum*. It is the Islamic influence, from the Persian (Sassanid) and

The Koutoubia mosque, Marrakech

23

Abbasid dynasties, that affects the ornamentation, in particular the rectangular brick patterns of projecting and receding bricks. These were reproduced in mud or *pisé* by the Berbers, who lacked the skills needed for brickwork (although a fine example in brick can be seen on the Koutoubia minaret in Marrakech).

However, despite all these influences the kasbahs do deserve to be called solely Berber. They have no Persian domes, arches from Rome or circular ornamentation. Created to suit particular local requirements they are far more original than imitative.

ENVIRONMENTAL ISSUES

Trekking, by its very nature, tends to be less environmentally damaging than many other forms of tourism. Small-scale tourism, using local staff

and consuming local produce, can give significant economic benefits to an impoverished region such as the Atlas mountains. Nonetheless, adhering to a few simple guidelines should help to reduce adverse impacts on the mountain environment.

Firstly, pack all litter out with you. Anyone carrying tins of food or bottles of water into the mountains has no excuse for not carrying the empty containers back out again. In recent years the area around the Toubkal refuge has become an eyesore, with large quantities of non-biodegradeable refuse lying around. A British trekking company ran a clean-up trek here, but such efforts will be in vain if people continue to jettison their garbage in this way.

Secondly, consider what form of fuel you will be using. Fuel for cooking fires has contributed substantially

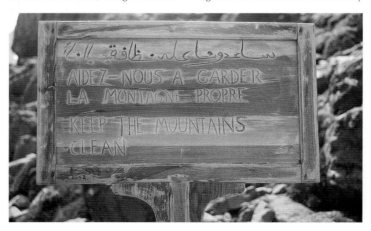

Rubbish on the Toubkal trail

to deforestation in the Atlas mountains. The resultant bare hillsides bear testimony to this ongoing process. Wherever possible, pack in fuel in the form of refillable gas bottles. This is especially the case for a group, where it is both cost effective and practical.

Always respect natural water sources and avoid any activities in their vicinity that may cause pollution. Be particularly careful to dispose of human waste at least 50m away from any water source.

USING THIS BOOK

The walking times given for routes described in this book allow for brief rests, but do not include lunch stops. However, the times specified are fairly generous. Much of the walking I have done in Morocco has been with large groups, some of whom have not

been particularly fit, and times are based on such groups. A fit party or individual would have no trouble fitting more into their schedule than is outlined in the book.

Each route is categorised as 'easy', 'moderate' or 'strenuous'. This refers solely to the amount of effort expended. However, because of the rocky terrain of the Atlas Mountains, some indication of the degree of seriousness is also given, where appropriate.

Where a route involves scrambling, exposure, climbing or any other significant hazards, these are mentioned alongside details of time and height gain. Other significant hazards could include the route being affected by early season snow or passing through remote terrain.

All route descriptions, and corresponding timings, relate to summer conditions. In winter and spring, snow cover will make any of the scree routes much quicker and easier (such as the ascent of Toubkal), but may block passes and prevent access by mule.

The directions L (left) and R (right) in the route instructions refer to the walker's direction of travel, unless stated otherwise.

As regards place names, those that appear on the 1:50,000 and 1:100,000 maps are used in the guide. Where these differ between maps the more popular (usually older) name is used.

All prices given are those found in 2003, at an exchange rate of 15.8 dirhams (dh) to £1; thus 1 dirham is equivalent to about 6 pence.

GETTING THERE

Air

Since the publication of the last edition, the good news for travellers is that Marrakech has now become a low-cost airline destination. Thomsonfly (www.thomsonfly.co.uk) offer direct flights from Luton and Manchester, from around £4 (!) + taxes one-way. This seems guaranteed to increase the region's popularity. There are also flights to Marrakech via Casablanca daily from London with:

Royal Air Maroc
www.royalairmaroc.co.uk
reservations tel. 020 7439 4361
These cost about £300 (inclusive of tax).

British Airways' subsidiary,

GB Airways
tel. 0845 773 3377,

also flies daily to Casablanca and twice weekly to Marrakech. There are sometimes bargains available, and in budget-airline style they offer one-way tickets, which could be useful if combining a trek with an overland tour. Air France also flies this route, via Paris, and is a good bet for travel from mainland Europe. On current timetables, any of these options sees the traveller arriving in Marrakech around 11pm. A cheaper alternative can be to find a charter flight to Agadir. There are international airports in Tangier, Fez, Casablanca and Rabat as well as Marrakech.

Another cheap way to get to Morocco, if time allows, is to find a cheap charter flight to Malaga, then to take a bus to Algeciras (2–3 hours, 8.70 Euros), from where a ferry runs to Tangier (3 hours, 23 Euros one way). A more expensive fast ferry also does the trip once daily. Having arrived in Tangier, take a taxi (40dh) to the rail station for the overnight train to Marrakech. This costs 220dh, plus 70dh for a sleeper berth, departing Tangier at 10.30 p.m. and arriving Marrakech at 8 a.m. Returning, the sleeper leaves Marrakech at 9 p.m., arriving 6 a.m. in Tangier. With a cheap flight from a regional UK airport, using this method it is still possible to leave home in the morning and arrive refreshed in Marrakech the next morning, with a considerable cost saving.

Overland

With the advent of cheap charter flights, overland travel has been largely superseded. It is a long train journey, taking around three days to reach Marrakech from London. It may, however, be worthwhile for someone travelling with an Inter-rail pass. Long-distance buses operate a regular service to Malaga, from where the local bus and ferry can be taken as described above. Buses also run from Paris and Brussels to Marrakech and other Moroccan cities.

Worth noting for anyone seeking a greener alternative to flying is the new high-speed rail line to Malaga. When completed, this will mean a 2hr 15mins journey from Madrid to Malaga. Connecting with the other high-speed lines to Barcelona and through France could slash journey times, and ultimately offer a real alternative, in time if not in price.

Ferry

Ferry crossings to Morocco run from Algeciras to Tangier and Ceuta (the latter being a Spanish enclave on the north Moroccan coast). The normal ferry to Tangier takes 3hrs, while the high-speed ferry takes 1½hrs. There is also a ferry to Tangier from Tarifa, the southernmost town in Spain. One other possibility is the ferry from Malaga to Melilla, another Spanish enclave situated well to the east of Tangier and Ceuta. It is a long crossing, and the ferry deposits you slightly out of the way for easy access to Marrakech. Finally, there is a ferry from Sète in southern France to Tangier (38 hours; runs every four days).

With all the above modes of transport prices change and you are advised to shop around for the best bargain.

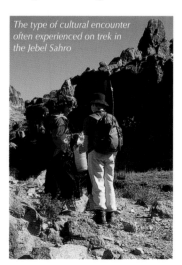

The type of cultural encounter often experienced on trek in the Jebel Sahro

TRAVEL WITHIN THE COUNTRY

Rail

Morocco has a relatively modern rail network which, while not extensive, is cheap and fairly comfortable. Trains run from Tangier via Rabat and Casablanca to Marrakech (see 'Air' section above for details of the sleeper train from Tangier).

Bus

There is an excellent bus network throughout Morocco at both local and long-distance level. Buses are invariably crowded; however, long-distance buses between the major cities are usually air conditioned and comfortable. Buses are usually the

The local camion which provides access to the Bougoumez valley (Mgoun area)

cheapest method of transport (other than hitching).

Taxi

There are two types of taxi within cities: *petit taxis* and *grand taxis*. The *petit taxis* take three passengers maximum, and most are fitted with meters. You would be advised to ensure that the meter is switched on; if it isn't, either ask the driver to turn it on or negotiate a price before your journey starts. If there is any argument, simply get out. Fares at night are 50 per cent higher.

Grand taxis nominally hold five people. They are not metered, and rates are twice those of the *petit taxis*. Unlike the *petit taxis*, however, they can operate on long-distance trips. It is essential to negotiate rates for such a trip beforehand. In addition there are the service (*collectif*) taxis. These operate on fixed routes between both cities and rural destinations, and depart when the taxi is full. Often they are just large taxis, but sometimes they may be pick-up trucks. They are much cheaper than *petit taxis* and operate in areas where there is no conventional bus service.

Car

Driving in Morocco is not without its headaches. The principal routes owe their existence to the French and are well surfaced, although even here an oncoming truck or bus may force you onto the hard shoulder. This consists of dirt and gravel, and the edge is often very pot-holed. Elsewhere the tracks are variable in quality, although those with a four-wheel-drive vehicle may be pleasantly surprised at how extensive the network of motorable tracks is.

Other hazards include fallen rocks (very common) and wandering animals. The Moroccans have a habit of surrounding a broken-down vehicle with large stones and then leaving the stones when the vehicle is towed away.

After reading the above, you may not feel much like hiring a car, but usually driving in Morocco passes without incident. The advantage of hire car, if you can afford it (it is expensive), is that you can travel quickly into remote areas. Comfort Plus rent-a-car in Marrakech, on Place de la Liberte (tel: 044 43 78 21, e-mail: comfort@iam.net.ma, website: www.comfortplus.ma), rents cars from 2100dh per week.

Petrol is cheaper in Morocco than in Britain – diesel is currently around 50 eurocents a litre – two-fifths the UK price.

Finally, a mention must be made of hitching. Under no circumstances try hitching if single and female. For men, hitching is usually very easy, although common sense dictates that care should be exercised, so keep hold of your baggage. You may well be expected to make a contribution to the driver on dismounting; this is accepted custom and should not be more than the equivalent local bus fare. Hitch-hiking is a recognised mode of transport in Morocco and is used frequently by locals.

VISA REQUIREMENTS

No visas are required for holders of a full UK visitor's passport. For other nationalities check with your embassy or travel agent.

To take a car to Morocco you need a national driving licence, together with an international driving permit (through Spain) and a 'green card' insurance certificate.

TRAVEL ADVICE

As Morocco is an Arab Muslim country, many potential visitors are inevitably concerned at being the target of anti-Western feeling. Currently there seems little evidence of bad feeling towards tourists, and no instances of violent attack. However, suicide bombings have occurred in Casablanca, directed against Morocco for its support of the US during the second Gulf War. The situation can change rapidly, in Morocco as in other countries, and any prospective visitor is recommended to monitor the Foreign Office website: www.fco.gov.uk. This is regularly updated with specific destination warnings for travellers. The CIA website performs a similar function, and may be more appropriate for US travellers to consult.

Tourism is vital to the Moroccan economy, and the authorities are keen to reassure and encourage visitors by, for example, clearing up touting blackspots.

SLEEPING AND EATING

Accommodation

In summer many people are happy to camp while trekking or simply to use a bivvy bag and sleep out. A tent gives some privacy and security, and provides a welcome haven from any rain, which is most likely to fall during afternoon thunderstorms.

The populous nature of the Atlas means that one is usually never very far from a village or *azib* (summer hut). Accommodation can nearly always be found in a village house, for a small charge. This often presents a delightful insight into the Berber way of life, and every visitor to the region should spend at least one night in a village house. They are normally fairly clean, if primitive; an unlucky guest may encounter the occasional flea. Toilet facilities can be poor or absent.

Within the Toubkal region, the Club Alpin Francais (CAF) maintains a series of mountain huts (see The Toubkal Region, Mountain Refuges, below, for location). All the huts provide mattress accommodation and cooking facilities. Guardians will provide meals at Imlil, the Toubkal hut, Tacheddirt and the chalet at Oukaimeden ski centre, but not at the Lepiney. Fanta and Coca-Cola can nearly always be purchased at these huts.

Depending on refuge and season, rates in 2003 were from 52 to 130dh per night. Discounts are available to CAF, Alpine Club and Austrian Alpine Club members on production of membership card. www.cafmaroc.co.ma is a useful site, giving details of all refuges and suggested summer and winter itineraries.

Note that the Lepiney hut is locked when not in use. In winter the *azibs* used on the circuit described are also abandoned and frequently buried under snow. A tent is therefore

The first 'bad step' in the Tessaout gorge –the route takes the left-hand side of the waterfall (Mgoun)

necessary if one ventures away from the villages and Toubkal refuge (see The Toubkal Region, Mountain Refuges, below).

Food on Trek

The staple diet of the Berbers consists of *tajine*, a stew of vegetables and mutton cooked in a conical eathenware pot. *Cous-cous*, a mix of vegetables and meat served with semolina, is also commonly eaten. If travelling singly or in a pair it is often possible to eat in village houses. Bear in mind, though, that it is largely a subsistence economy and there is thus little surplus. When passing through villages it is usually possible to buy bread, eggs and the occasional onion or potato. Beyond this it is wisest to come supplied with provisions bought in Marrakech. What little fresh food there is is often exorbitantly priced – I have been charged £5 for a small marrow! In autumn the situation is better – fresh apples and walnuts are available in the lower villages at reasonable prices.

A few villages have little stores which have a remarkably uniform line in stock. As Morocco is one of the world's largest sardine exporters it is not surprising to find shelves full of these. Biscuits, Moroccan tea, soft drinks and tins of olives form the bulk of the remaining stock. Several of the shops also sell cooking oil, nuts, powdered milk, Vache Qui Rit processed cheese and tinned fruit.

It is worth mentioning another dish one may encounter if invited into a Berber home. Apart from copious quantities of mint tea, a *mechwi* may be served on special occasions. This consists of large pieces of barbecued lamb, with a whole sheep being consumed on special occasions.

Cooking

Where there is no other fuel available for fires, wood has to be collected from distant hillsides by the local

Out of the main towns, Moroccan villages can be very basic

Approaching Imhilene

inhabitants. In the villages the most common sort of fuel is Butagaz. Unfortunately the cylinders are too large to contemplate carrying, but if you have hired a mule, they are ideal. The bottles are cheap to purchase and refill and are freely exchangeable. The initial cylinders are best purchased in Marrakech, together with a screw-in burner attachment (very cheap).

Note: when buying gas, make sure you do not get camping gaz, as the cylinders are not exchangeable in the mountains. A better option for a small group is camping gaz stoves with disposable cartouches. Whatever backpacking stove you choose, fuel will have to be bought in Marrakech.

Finally, in the Toubkal region you could get by with using the gas in the refuges, and either eating in - village houses or living on cold food for the rest of the time (no problem in summer). Mint tea is usually available.

WHAT TO TAKE

Do not be fooled by the proximity to the Sahara or the temperatures in Marrakech; it often gets cold high in the mountains.

Parties visiting until the end of June should ensure they each have an ice-axe. Crampons are also essential for winter and early spring, and advisable until late June.

In summer, lightweight clothes are needed for the valleys, while a warm sweater and waterproof jacket should be carried for the peaks. Autumn and spring need the addition of woolly hat and gloves, plus another jersey. Winter necessitates full cold-weather gear, with mountain boots, gaiters and preferably a duvet jacket.

33

As regards footwear a pair of lightweight hiking boots will suffice, except when crampons need to be worn. Boots with canvas uppers are ideal – they do not need to be watertight. Gaiters or, even better, stop-touts, are useful on the long scree descents.

The ultra-violet is very intense in Morocco, and an adequate supply of high-factor sunscreen and glacier cream should be carried. Likewise good sunglasses, or snow goggles in early season, should be worn. A sunhat is essential during the summer months.

With regard to sleeping bags, a lightweight bag is adequate during summer. Winter bivvies clearly necessitate a four-season bag.

Tents are a matter of choice – in summer it is nice to sleep under the stars, though even at this time of year torrential rain can be expected occasionally. A good compromise is a Gore-tex or similar bivvy bag.

An adequate supply of water puri-fying tablets is essential. These are unobtainable in Morocco. Disposable wet wipes are also useful.

There is abundant scrambling and many alpine-style ridges; those who are competent may wish to take a rope and basic rock gear (several krabs, slings and belt or harness). Add-itionally the circuit of the Mgoun mas-sif includes an optional gorge walk that involves some climbing: rope and basic gear are required for this.

For cooking equipment, see Sleeping and Eating, above.

34

HEALTH MATTERS

There are no compulsory vaccinations for Morocco, though those for polio, tetanus, typhoid and cholera are strongly advised. Also recommended is an injection against hepatitis A.

Malaria is prevalent in Morocco, supposedly only in the lowland areas of the far south-west of the country. Some people take prophylactic tablets; most don't. I have never heard of anyone contracting malaria in the Atlas mountains.

Bilharzia is a risk in parts of Morocco, though once again it is not known to occur in the High Atlas. It may be a risk in areas such as the Jebel Sahro, however, and the visitor is advised to exercise caution. Avoid wading or standing in still water if possible. **Under no circumstances should water be drunk without first sterilising with tablets or by boiling.**

The most common complaint is **diarrhoea**. This can be caused simply by a change of diet or, more likely, by the poor hygiene standards. Treatments such as Imodium or Lomotil are recommended as part of the medical kit, as are a few sachets of rehydrating salts, such as Dioralyte. More serious diarrhoea may need to be treated with antibiotics. If it persists, seek medical attention. I have never heard of any cases of amoebic dysentery, although the lack of hygiene would suggest this is a possibility.

Hepatitis A can also be picked up by travellers in the region, and is associated with poor hygeine. Potential visitors may want to consider an injection of Gamma Globulin prior to departure. Consult your doctor or travel clinic to establish what is the current best form of prevention for this disease.

Visitors staying in village houses run the risk of contracting **ringworm**. This fungal infection causes characteristic circular inflamed red patches on the skin and scalp, and may be initially confused with reaction to insect bites. It is contagious, though

A fine example of a small agadir, Tessaout valley (Mgoun)

not serious. If you contract it, do not share clothes and towels, and avoid direct skin contact with others. It is easily treated with an ointment such as Daktarin.

While **Acute Mountain Sickness** cannot be ruled out, it is very unlikely. This can be fatal, often in cases when the condition is not diagnosed accurately. The cure is extremely simple – return to a lower altitude immediately. Symptoms include severe fatigue, headaches, nausea and possibly fainting fits. All of these could be experienced by an unfit trekker suddenly exposed to the rigours of Morocco; if in doubt descend. Toubkal and the other mountains will still be there when you have acclimatised. Mild symptoms of altitude sickness such as headaches, general listlessness and loss of appetite may occur, particularly on the typical ascent of Toubkal, undertaken within two days of leaving Marrakech.

Heat causes problems to those unused to it, so ensure that plenty of liquids are consumed. Problems of **dehydration** will be exacerbated if the person is suffering from an upset stomach.

EMERGENCY SERVICES

There are no official rescue organisations serving the Atlas mountains. All CAF huts possess a stretcher, first aid box and manual (but note that certain huts, such as Lepiney refuge, are

normally locked). Assistance in getting help is usually available, since the mountains are heavily populated. Evacuation by mule is easy to arrange, if the patient is in a fit state to travel. In more serious cases evacuation by helicopter is possible (there is one stationed at Marrakech). The nearest telephones in the Toubkal region are at Oukaimeden and Imlil/Aroumd, where there are blue *teleboutiques*. Mobile telephones greatly increase the ease of contact; reception is available at the Toubkal refuge, but elsewhere in the mountains it is difficult to predict network coverage. Contact police in the first instance. In the Toubkal region, the Imlil Bureau des Guides will also be able to advise.

MAPS AND WHERE TO OBTAIN THEM

The whole of the Atlas and Anti-Atlas have been mapped at 1:100,000 scale, published in a series since 1970. In addition, the Toubkal region is covered by a 1:50,000 scale map, published in 1968.

These maps both suffer from a degree of inaccuracy and a lack of detail. The 1:100,000 series lacks many of the names of passes, peaks and spot heights. It does, however, have relief and is easy to interpret. Contours exist, but are generally impossible to read. The 1:50,000 maps, while obviously more detailed, are difficult to read as most contour heights are unmarked, and rocky areas are confusing. Nevertheless they are the best available and should be adequate for walking purposes.

The following maps cover the areas in this guide.

- **Toubkal region:** Jbel Toubkal (1:50,000), Oukaimeden-Toubkal (1:100,000). These 1:100,000 maps also cover the extreme western and southern corners of the Toubkal region – Amizmiz (W), Tizi-n'Test (SW), Taliwine (S).

- **Mgoun area:** unfortunately the Mgoun massif overlaps the corners of four 1:100,000 maps! They are: Azilal (NW), Zawyat Ahancal (NE), Qalaa't Mgouna (SE), Skoura (SW).

Telouat (Feuille no. NH 29 XXIII 2) links the Oukaimeden-Toubkal and Skoura maps, thus providing information for anyone wishing to undertake a traverse between the two regions.

- **Jebel Sahro:** on the 1:100,000 series, Tazzarine covers the bulk of the region, while Boumalne (Feuille no. NH 30 XIX 1) covers the northern fringes, including the important centre of Iknion. Ait Youl and the western fringes are on the Qalaa't Mgouna map (Feuille no. NH 29 XXIV 2).

Unfortunately, in recent years the availability of all maps in Morocco has steadily declined and they are now very scarce. Even maps formerly displayed in hotels and *gîtes* have been removed in the name of

On the approach to Tassgdelt Tamaigalt

security. The relevant government agency is unlikely to help with requests in person for maps. This entails several days' wait in Rabat, only (in all likelihood) to have the request refused. Guides sometimes obtain limited stock and these may be available in the Hotel Ali in Marrakech or in Imlil. The price per sheet in 2003 was 140dh.

In Britain **Stanfords** (12–13 Long Acre, London WC2E 9LP, tel: 0207 836 1321, website: www.stanfords. co.uk) periodically stock a set of four copied 1:100,000 maps which cover the Toubkal area, namely: Amezmiz; Tizi-n'Test; Taliwine; and Oukaimeden-Toubkal. This set of four costs £16, and should suffice for most trekkers. The Taliwine map in this collection also covers Jebel Sirwa. West Col productions produce a useful 1:100,000 map-guide of the Mgoun area, which comes complete with route descriptions and other information. Available also from Stanfords.

The **Map Shop** (tel. 0800 085 40 80, website: www.themapshop. co.uk) also stocks the four 1:100,000 Toubkal area set.

Atlas Maps (tel/fax: 01592 873546; not available March–May) can usually help with any published Atlas areas at all scales and may have maps to sell.

The **Alpine Club Library** has a file of Atlas maps.

In Morocco the maps are supplied by a government agency, the Ministere de l'Agriculture et de la Reforme Agraire (Division de la Carte), Rabat, but note the problems involved (above).

INTERACTING WITH LOCAL PEOPLE

The Berbers of the Atlas mountains have a largely self-sufficient way of life, with little reliance on the outside world. A consequence of this is that most Berbers have very little money with which to buy luxuries or necessary tools. A European tourist therefore represents a big potential source of income to them. This is now the case in the Toubkal region, where tourism plays a large part of the local economy. In common with much tourism, the interaction between visitor and local has had some negative impacts. Tourists' visible wealth means the Berbers invariably try to overcharge for whatever service or goods they provide. It is important to bargain for everything. When passing through a village, you may sometimes be pestered by children asking for sweets and money. Anything but a refusal will encourage further begging – which is directed only at tourists. Adults occasionally ask for money, cigarettes and aspirin which, in the absence of medical facilities, serves as a universal panacea. Another situation the trekker commonly experiences are the invitations to eat, or drink tea, only to be presented with a bill afterwards.

A general rule, and one which avoids much hassle, is to negotiate the

Snake charmer,
Djemaa el Fna

price of any purchase or service beforehand, whether this be food, accommodation or tea. If you fail to do this and are subsequently over-charged, remember that prices start from a very low base, and the disputed amount is not worth spoiling your holiday for.

The above negatives, once acknowledged, quickly assume little significance, and the visitor is able to gain much from meeting locals. Outside of commercial transactions the Berbers are usually very friendly and well mannered. Theft is rare, and on trek possessions are safe in their hands. It is worth establishing what food is shared on trek, as items such as coffee and jam are real luxuries and will be rapidly consumed otherwise.

Berbers are excellent linguists. Besides their own unwritten language and Arabic many also speak French. Only a few, however, speak English.

Do not miss hearing some Berber music with its very African rhythm and complicated drumming. The singing takes the form of call and response and the overall effect is an exciting, distinctive sound. There are opportunities to hear such singing at the 'Moussem' in the first week of September at Aroumd (a large festival in honour of Sidi [St] Chamarouch).

Finally the Aid el-Kebir, or festival of the sheep, is an important celebra-tion. Moslem rather than Berber, it celebrates Abraham's willingness to sacrifice Isaac and lasts three days. On the first day each family slaughters a sheep or goat, after first dressing in white. In Atlas villages such as Aroumd a costume is stitched together from fresh goat skins in preparation for the next day. The costumes are worn by the two most eligible young males in the village. They present a bizarre spectacle as they run around the

39

village, chasing everyone who emerges from their house. This game of hide and seek continues all day. On the evening of the second day the head male of each household tells the history of the family going back for generations. This oral tradition is believed to be pre-Islamic in origin. Like Ramadan, the date of this festival varies from year to year.

MULE HIRE AND LOCAL GUIDES
Mule Hire
The absence of supplies, distance from roadheads and general lack of facilities mean that all equipment must be carried while on trek. By far the easiest way of doing this is to hire mules. The Atlas are criss-crossed with a network of mule trails. This, together with the low cost, makes mule hire an attractive option.

The usual arrangement is that you hire the mule; the muleteer who accompanies it does not charge for his services. In the Toubkal area each mule has its own muleteer; in other areas a muleteer may look after two or three mules.

Rates are around 100dh per day. On top of this it is customary, if on a trek, either to provide food for the muleteers or to give them money to buy their own. Expect to pay around 30–40dh per muleteer per day.

All rates should be negotiated beforehand, as should food arrange-ments for the muleteers. Frequently, unless otherwise agreed, the muleteers will arrive in camp foodless and expect to share your supplies. This obviously plays havoc with your planning.

At the end of each trek it is cus-tomary to give a *cadeau* equivalent to

Hiring mules makes life easier on trek

Porters and their mules approaching the gold mine of Tiouit (Jebel Sahro)

one day's wages to each muleteer (i.e. the cost of a day's mule hire). Tips are officially illegal in Morocco, so this is disguised as a gift.

The mules and muleteers move very fast over the ground; irrespective of your level of fitness, you would find it hard to keep up. Consequently they usually depart well after the trekkers. It is advisable to carry a packed lunch, as on a typical day the mules will overtake you in the early afternoon. Mint tea will be brewing by the time you arrive.

Local Guides

Undoubtedly on your arrival in Imlil you will be importuned by people offering their services as guides; they are unlikely to be official mountain guides, but will certainly have a knowledge of all the valleys and passes. However, with the aid of this book, it shouldn't be necessary to hire a guide. This is particularly true if you

are hiring mules – the muleteers will perform the function.

Visitors to Jebel Sahro may wish to hire a guide. Beware of rogues. It is often difficult to tell in advance, but if in doubt never hire a guide who does not live in the area. Official guides will have their status shown on their ID card.

Anyone wishing to hire an official guide can contact the Moroccan Office de Tourisme in Marrakech (Place Abd el-Moumen ben Ali, Gueliz) or, for the Toubkal region, the Bureau des Guides in Imlil (tel: 00212 44 48 56 04, fax: 00212 44 48 56 22, mobile: 062 15 41 89, e-mail: Toudaoui@hotmail.com). Brahim Toudaoui there speaks good English and is very helpful.

The going rate for an official guide is 250dh per day; these guides are trained in mountaincraft and are much more reliable than the unofficial 'guides' who offer their services.

While the latter may know the area, they are unlikely to be experienced enough to lead groups over steep or snowy ground.

Porters: Until June, or even later, many of the high passes (such as Tizi-n'Ouanoums) are impassable by mule. In these circumstances it is necessary to hire porters. Each porter will carry about 25 kilos. Porters' rates are cheaper than those for mule hire but, obviously, they can carry much less. Hiring a porter can be arranged in larger villages such as Imlil.

MARRAKECH

Marrakech is one of the country's four imperial cities and its former capital (its name and 'Morocco' share the same origin). At least a thousand years old, it first became a town of importance during the Almoravid dynasty in the 11th century. It was during this period that the first Koutoubia mosque was built. The minaret (of later date) still dominates the skyline of Marrakech and makes a useful central reference point.

Marrakech is invariably the starting point for trips to the Toubkal region, clearly visible from the city during the winter months. It is also the best starting point for visits to the Mgoun area and Jebel Sahro. A comprehensive guide to the city is outside the scope of this book, but it is the arrival point in Morocco for most trekkers, and negotiating this often bewildering city is aided by some prior knowledge.

The city can roughly be divided into two parts: the old part, within the medieval ramparts, is known as the Medina; the modern French quarter is

The first rain in 4 months, Marrakech

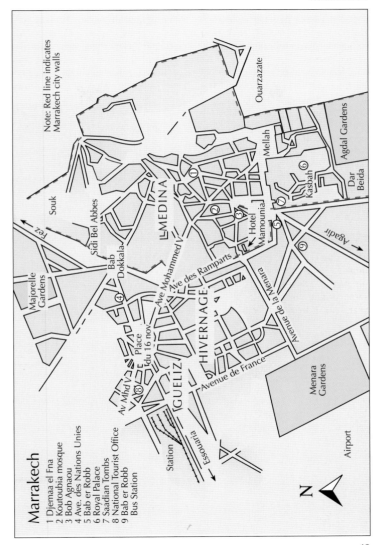

Marrakech

1 Djemaa el Fna
2 Koutoubia mosque
3 Bob Agnaou
4 Ave. des Nations Unies
5 Bab er Robb
6 Royal Palace
7 Saadian Tombs
8 National Tourist Office
9 Bab er Robb Bus Station

Note: Red line indicates
Marrakech city walls

Ouarzazate

Agdal Gardens

Dar Beida

Mellah

Kasbah

Hotel Mamounia

Agadir

L MEDINA

Souk

Sidi Bel Abbes

Fez

Bab Dokkala

Majorelle Gardens

Ave Mohammed V

Ave des Ramparts

HIVERNAGE

Av Mhd V

Place du 16 nov

GUELIZ

Avenue de la Menara

Avenue de France

Station

Essouaria

Menara Gardens

Airport

N

43

called Gueliz. Within the Medina there is an enormous souk – a labyrinth of small shops and narrow alleyways where it is very easy to get lost. The souk is bordered on its south side by a square, the Djemaa el Fna (literally 'meeting place of the dead'). This is the main focal-point for entertainment in Marrakech. In the evenings this square comes alive with acrobats, fortune tellers, fire-eaters and dancers, while smoke billows

Inside the souk, Marrakech

Tilework, Marrakech

from dozens of snack tables serving all manner of food under bright lights. Although some of the acts are certainly there for Western tourists, the bulk of them are intended for Moroccans (this is particularly true of the storytellers). A visit here is an absolute 'must' while in Marrakech. Sit and observe it all from the relative peace of one of the cafe terraces that border the square.

Marrakech has been notorious in the past for hustlers, 'guides' and others who would relentlessly pursue tourists. This was clearly beginning to affect the tourist trade, and the government responded by introducing a law forbidding such harassment. It is now very noticeable that you can wander freely around the souk and take your time – a pleasure rather than the ordeal it was a few years ago. Visitors are still exposed to numerous hassles, though. Overcharging in cafes and restaurants, and aggressive demands for unrealistic sums of money when taking photos in the Djemaa el Fna are common experiences. A swindle which I experienced on my most recent visit was on arrival at a hotel late at night – a time when most visitors are disorientated. Paying for a 190dh room in advance with a 200dh note, the clerk distracted me, produced a 50dh note on the counter, and then demanded the 'extra' 140dh. Fortunately I knew I only had 200dh notes on me, and the original note was quickly 'found' on the floor behind the desk. The message for travellers is to be aware that such swindles occur, and do not to be afraid to stand your ground when you suspect something is amiss.

Within the medina, Marrakech

Getting Around

From the airport a *petit taxi* to the city centre is 80–100dh. The price is displayed on noticeboards and should also be on the taxi windscreen.

The main local bus station is located outside the Bab er Robb gate, south-south-east from the Djemaa el Fna, 20–30mins walk. *Petit taxis* in the city are cheap; don't worry if they are already occupied, the driver will usually stop for you. Mention should also be made of the horse-drawn carriages or *caleches* that are a feature of Marrakech. By no means there solely for the tourist trade, they are used by Marrakchis as taxis. They are slower than, but a similar price to, *petit taxis*.

Accommodation

This ranges from the lowest flea-pit in the Medina to world-class hotels like the Mamounia. There is a decent patrolled campsite near the new quarter on the edge of the city. It is best to take a taxi there. For cheap hotels look in the streets immediately south of the Djemaa el Fna, across from the Souk. There are numerous small hotels centred around courtyards. Of these, Hotel Essouaria comes recommended. It is worth asking to see the room before handing over your passport; often this will ensure you are not then given the worst room in the hotel. Hotel Ali near the Djemaa el Fna, facing the Place Foucauld garden, is a popular base for trekkers. The Hotel CMT, directly

on the Fna, is cheap and popular.

The Hotel Foucauld is situated 300m from the Djemaa el Fna on Ave. el Mouahidine, near the Koutoubia. A popular place with tour groups over the years, the income has not been re-invested. The place now feels distinctly shabby, and tour groups have deserted it. It is run by unpleasant counter staff, and can't be recommended.

More upmarket hotels tend to be centred around the new town, athough a few very classy *riads*, traditional Medina houses, are now appearing on the scene – ideal if you want to feel part of the local scene.

After a tiring trek, there is something to be said for splashing out on a nice hotel, and a good option is to stay around the Place de la Liberte, just outside the city walls and an easy walk to the Djemaa el Fna. Hotel de La Menara does double rooms at 450dh and has a nice swimming pool and bar. Further upmarket is the nearby Hotel Le Marrakech (also with a swimming pool), with double rooms around 600dh. If you just want to use the hotel pool, this is open to non-residents for 100dh.

Finally, a nice hotel is the Hotel Mousaffir, right next to the train station, again with a swimming pool, for 400dh (double room). It is part of the French-owned Ibis chain, so of a predictably clean nature.

There is also a youth hostel in Marrakech, situated a few streets south of the railway station. It is arguable whether this is worth

Pottery stalls, Marrakech

considering, given the low cost of the centrally located budget hotels.

Supplies

For all treks, it is advisable to buy provisions in Marrakech, where there is a greater variety and reasonable prices. The big produce markets and main grocery shops both in the Medina and the Gueliz (new town) display prices. A taxi between old and new towns costs only 10–15dh, and the bus, No. 1, costs under 1dh.

Note: it is not possible to change money in the mountains, ensure that you change sufficient in Marrakech!

Leaving Marrakech

The main bus station is the Bab Doukkala, situated on the north-west edge of the old city walls, reached by heading north-east from the Place de la Liberte. Go here for buses and shared taxis to Azilal, Ait Mohamed, the Souss and Dades valley, and any other Moroccan city. However, buses to Asni and the Toubkal region depart from a new bus station well out on the Asni–Tizi-n'Test road, most easily reached by *petit taxi*. On foot, pass the Bab Agnaou and through the Bab er Robb, turning right at once to walk out to the roundabout on the city walls ring road. Then continue straight on for a further 10mins. There are buses from here to Asni at least eight times daily, price 20dh. It is 20dh by shared taxi, which run frequently (1hr Marrakech–Asni).

The train station is situated on the Essaouira road, with the Supatours bus station alongside, and is most easily reached by *petit taxi*.

THE TOUBKAL REGION

This area, containing all the highest peaks, is by far the most popular region in the Atlas for walkers. The trek up to Toubkal and the Neltner hut is undertaken each year by several thousand visitors of all nationalities. It is in some ways atypical of the Atlas trekking experience, being an area of stark volcanic peaks, rather than the usual limestone scenery found elsewhere. Architecturally, too, the area is less interesting than the Mgoun area and its kasbahs. Nonetheless, with North Africa's highest mountain and its proximity to Marrakech, the area deserves its popularity. Roughly speaking, the Toubkal area is bounded by the Tizi-n'Test to the west and the Tizi-n'Tichka to the east. Most of the interest is concentrated in or around the central line of peaks, from Ouanoukrim north-east to Annrhemer and Angour.

ACCESS

The area is invariably approached from Marrakech, taking the Tizi-n'Test road as far as Asni. Asni has an interesting Saturday souk, garage, shops, *teleboutiques* and a postbox. There is a spartan but clean hostel in an olive grove by the river (no cooking facilities, but there are plenty of eating places by the souk). The nearby hotel seems permanently closed. In spring, when there is too much snow on the high peaks for walking, there is a rewarding walk up on to the Kik plateau from Asni. This is botanically very interesting, and provides superb views of the main Atlas chain.

THE MIZANE VALLEY: IMLIL AND AROUMD

This is far and away the most frequented of the bases for exploring the mountains.

Imlil (1740m)

A large village situated at the end of the motor road, 17km from Asni. As it is the standard approach route for those wishing to climb Toubkal it is well geared to

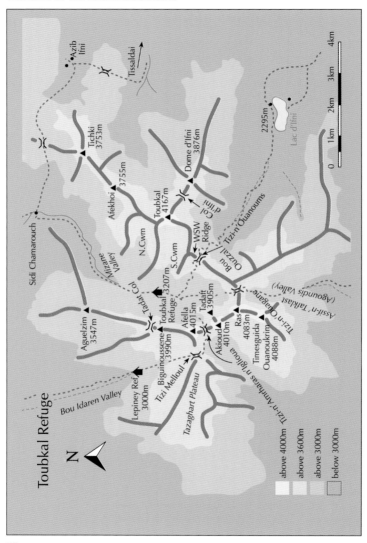

Toubkal Refuge

N

Bou Idaren Valley

Lepiney Ref 3000m

Biguinoussene 3990m

Tizi Melloul

Tazaghart Plateau

Aguelzim 3547m

Sidi Chamarouch

Tajat Col

Mizane Valley

N.Cwm

S.Cwm

Toubkal Refuge 3207m

Afella 4015m

Akioud 4010m

Tadaft 3905m

Ras 4083m

Timesguida Ouanoukrim 4088m

Tizi-n'Ouagane

Tizi-n'Amrharas n'Iglioua

Assif-n' Tarlkast (Agoundis Valley)

Tizi-n'Ouanoums

Bou Ouzzal

Col d'Ifni

WSW Ridge

Toubkal 4167m

Atekhoi 3755m

Tichki 3753m

N.Cwm

Dome d'Ifni 3876m

2295m

Lac d'Ifni

Azib Ifni

Tissaldai

above 4000m
above 3600m
above 3000m
below 3000m

0   1km   2km   3km   4km

Ouanoukrim from the
foot of the Tizi-
n'Ouanoums

supplying trekkers' needs. It is a village dependant upon mule rather than motor transport, and the many mule stalls give the place a 'Wild West' feel. There are several shops selling drinks, tinned foods, sweets and biscuits. In addition there is a *teleboutique*, a few simple restaurants and the inevitable souvenir stalls. Of importance to the trekker are a few grocers selling a range of fresh fruit and vegetables, and a bakery. Shops here sell both the 1:50,000 and 1:100,000 scale maps of the area.

Adjoining the main square is the CAF refuge. This is spacious and comfortable, with a small camping area. The building is clean inside with a dining-room, kitchen (gas and all utensils), showers and bunk beds with foam mattresses. For 2003 rates see Mountain Refuges section below.

There are several pleasant, low-priced *gîtes* in Imlil, while several grades up is the Etoile du Toubkal. Roomsare 150dh B+B, 200dh half-board, and there is a restaurant/café area downstairs. You can also change money here.

In recent years Imlil has moved upmarket with the opening of the Kasbah du Toubkal, a luxurious former summer home of a *caid*. This is situated on the hill over-looking Imlil, 10mins walk away. It is fitted with local materials and was used as a location for Martin Scorsese's film *Kundun*. Cost varies depending on room, but expect to pay from 140dh upwards (Kasbah du Toubkal, BP 31, Imlil, Asni, tel. 01883 744 392).

Springtime, Aroumd

Imlil is the best place to arrange mules for transporting baggage. Theoretically there are fixed rates for both mule and guide hire; in practice this never applies. If staying in the CAF refuge the guardian will assist in finding mules. *Gîte* owners can also organise mules and everything needed for a trek. Otherwise it is an easy matter to find someone willing to provide a mule. Negotiations are best conducted over a cup of mint tea in a nearby cafe. Be prepared to haggle.

What you pay for is the mule; the muleteer's service is included in the price. If it seems unnecessary to have one muleteer per mule bear in mind that each mule is worth around £500, a considerable sum to a villager and an investment that must be cared for. By and large the mules are well looked after in the mountains.

Expect to pay around 100dh a day per mule (2003 rates). On top of this a *cadeau* of one day's wages is expected by each muleteer. Remember that these prices are a guideline only, dependent upon your desire and ability to haggle. Remember also that when loading mules the Berbers will invariably try to supply one or two mules more than is necessary. Hiring of guides, if desired, is also easy in Imlil – check at the Bureau des Guides, in the square by the CAF refuge. (see Introduction, Mule Hire and Local Guides, for more information)

Getting there

From Marrakech buses run at least eight times a day to Asni. They depart from the Tizi-n'Test road (see Introduction, Leaving Marrakech) to Asni (about 1hr; fare is about 20dh). A shared taxi will do the journey in half the time, at the same price. From Asni take a service bus (often a pick-up truck) to Imlil (17km). This road is now asphalted, so service taxis often continue to Imlil from Marrakech; look out for these in Asni (fare about 20dh). Avoid being led away from the area in front of the souk in Asni, where the taxis deposit you, as this is the best place to pick up onward transport.

Aroumd (1960m) (also spelt Around, Aremd)

Situated 40mins walk up the valley from Imlil, Aroumd can also be reached by car via a rough track. Not visible from Imlil, Aroumd occupies the southern slopes of a huge landslip that is still virtually vegetation-free. An extensive area of terraced fields adjoins it.

In recent years the accommodation in Aroumd has been considerably upgraded. There are now several small *gîtes d'étape*, at around 32dh per night, and hot showers are even available for 10dh. Mule hire can also be arranged here. The village serves as the base for a British trekking company. Electricity and street lighting have also been introduced, and there is a blue *tele-boutique* on the other side of the river, shortly before the ford to the main village.

The Imenane Valley: Tacheddirt and Oukaimeden

This is the next valley east from the Mizane valley, and is separated from it by a long ridge which is crossed in several places by passes. It is a useful base for ascents of Angour and Annrhemer.

It is possible to drive into the upper Imenane valley from Imlil, although the road at present ends across the valley from Tacheddirt, the highest village. A car left here would be vulnerable, but there is a daily bus service. The best approach, therefore, is either to walk over from Imlil or Aguersioual (see Day 11, below). The latter approach, while longer, has the advantage of passing through the beautiful lower reaches of this valley.

Tacheddirt (2300m)

The only practical base in the valley. There is a CAF refuge here at the western end of the village, marked on the 1:50,000 map. More basic than the Imlil refuge, it sleeps 20. Cooking facilities are available, or the guardian can provide meals. Several *gîtes* have recently opened, which offer the visitor a chance to experience traditional Berber hospitality. There are no shops in the village, but bread, eggs and (possibly) vegetables in season are usually available. Mule hire can be arranged here. Campers should beware of scorpions.

Oukaimeden (2610m)

This is a small ski resort situated in a high basin northeast of Imlil. It is rather too far north for serving as a base for climbing Toubkal, though ideal for ascending Angour and visiting the upper Ourika valley. Oukaimeden has a telephone and a road connection with Marrakech.

Being a ski resort it is very quiet in summer, with only a few local herders around. Mule hire is therefore not feasible. Throughout summer there are one or two local shops open, selling the usual tinned goods at more than usually exorbitant prices. In winter there are several hotels and restaurants open.

Open throughout the year is the CAF refuge. This is a large building with the appearance of a chalet-hotel. Inside this initial impression is reinforced, there is a bar room, games room and even a bandstand! Additionally there are showers and good French food available.

An alternative is Chez Ju-Ju, a hotel/restaurant 100m further up the road. It is run by a French lady who has been here since just after the war. There is dormitory accommodation, with clean sheets, at a very reasonable charge, with hot showers included. The hotel offers breakfast with expresso coffee and, best of all, French cuisine. It is also the only place in the mountains where alcohol is served. Beer is served ice-cold and is extremely welcome in mid-summer. Chez Ju-Ju is open all year round, except during the month of Ramadan.

Getting there

Oukaimeden is connected to Marrakech by road. This road (signposted in Marrakech) leads via the Ourika valley, with plenty of hairpins, to Oukaimeden. An alternative, if driving, is to continue towards Asni. A mile beyond Tahannaout turn L along a signposted road – this route is very scenic. There is also a dirt road connecting Asni with Oukaimeden, used mainly by mine trucks. There is a bus service from Marrakech in winter, but in summer it is necessary to hire a *grand taxi*. Expect to pay a premium for taxis to here – around 300–400dh for the one-way journey from Marrakech. Hitching there is also easy, though occasionally slow.

PERIPHERAL BASES

Setti Fatma

Situated in the Ourika valley, at the eastern edge of the region, this is a base for some of the wildest and most remote regions of the Toubkal area. It is much less frequented than the Toubkal trail from Imlil.

Getting there

There are several buses (which are very slow) or, a better option, service taxis from Marrakech. It is also feasible to hitch; this is a popular destination for Moroccans. Follow the S513 as for Oukaimeden and continue along the main valley to Aghbalou (1011m), where there is a smart French restaurant. There is also a restaurant/hotel at Assgaour, 1km before Setti Fatma. The road continues to Setti Fatma, which is like a bigger version of Imlil. There are several shops and small Moroccan restaurants selling *tajine*, *brochettes*, etc, and several hotels – expect to pay around 100dh for a reasonable room. Mule hire is possible.

The reason for Setti Fatma's popularity with locals is the cascades, beautiful waterfalls 30mins' walk from the village which are well worth a visit. Setti Fatma also serves as a good base for ascending some of the outlying peaks (such as Taskka-n-Zat, Meltsen and Yagour – see under Outlying Summits, below) and crossing to south or east. From Setti Fatma to Timichchi (see Day 9, below) is 6–7 hours' walking up the main Ourika valley.

Tizi-n'Test

On the north (Asni) side of the pass the village of Ijoukak provides a good base for the westernmost peaks of the region. It is at the lower end of the Agoundis valley, which leads to the Tizi Melloul (see Day 2, below) or Tizi-n-Ouagane. Mule hire is possible, and several shops, meals and rooms are available. Several treks start or finish here. The Agoundis valley can be driven along to the village of Taghbart.

Southern Approaches

It is possible to reach the southern flanks of the Toubkal massif in several places via a dirt road. This can be useful in early season, obviating the need to cross steep snow on passes such as the Tizi-n'Ouanoums. Probably the best starting point is Amsouzart, a large village handily placed for Lac d'Ifni and Tissaldai.

Getting there

Amsouzart can be reached either from the Tizi n'Test or Tizi n'Tichka.

From Tizi n'Test: catch a bus from Marrakech via the Tizi n'Test to Aoulouz, on the P32. Shared taxis or Camions depart frequently to Amsouzart or Imlil, a larger village an hour's walk down the valley. Expect to pay around 50dh from Aoulouz to Amsouzart.

From Tizi n'Tichka: Catch any bus from Marrakech, or a shared taxi (departing from Bab Doukkala), heading towards Ouarzazate and get off at Agouim, a small market town on the southern side of the Tizi n'Tichka (cost about 50dh). From there, head west for 30km to

Sour, another market town, along a dirt road (soon to be asphalted?). There is a signpost in Agouim for Lac d'Ifni – this is the road you take. There is frequent traffic to and from Sour – take a bus or shared taxi from Agouim (about 30dh). A yellow Land Rover leaves from Sour to Amsouzart each afternoon, costing 50dh. The road is very slow and bumpy, but passes through some spectacular scenery on the southern flanks of the main Atlas range.

Many people hire a Land Rover in Marrakech or Ouarzazate and are driven up the Tifnoute valley to Amsouzart. The road up the Tifnoute is being upgraded.

MOUNTAIN REFUGES
People visiting the region often lack either the time or the desire to undertake a trek; the CAF refuges, however, make ideal bases for a short stay or for peak-bagging.

Costs for using the CAF refuges were as follows in 2003.

	CAF, Alpine Club members	Non-members
Toubkal (Neltner)		
1/5–31/10	40dh	80dh
1/11 – 30/4	80dh	130dh
Imlil, Tacheddirt	26dh	52dh
Tazaghart (Lepiney), Oukaimeden	32dh	64dh

A small reduction on the non-member rate is available to YHA members – take your card.

Toubkal (Neltner) Refuge (3207m)
By far the most frequently used of all the mountain refuges, its popularity is due largely to its situation at the

foot of Toubkal. It is open throughout the year, although new snow can make it harder to reach in winter. The original Neltner refuge was named after Louis Neltner, a French geologist and climber who helped raise money for its construction. Demand over the years exceeded capacity, though, and a new refuge was opened recently. This sleeps upward of 120 people, but can still get crowded. Hot showers are available for 10dh. There is a comfortable lounge area, and hot food is available from the guardian (about 30dh for *cous cous* or *tagine*).

A local entrepreneur is so confident of continuing growth in the market that he is building another refuge immediately below the new refuge. If nothing else, this may see prices fall due to competition.

Campers below the huts will be required to use the huts' facilities and thus improve the present insanitary conditions at the campsite.

Imlil to Toubkal Refuge

Time:	4¹/₂–5hrs
Ascent:	1470m
Grade:	strenuous

This is the standard approach, and the best-used path in the Atlas. From Imlil take the main track heading up from

Approaching the white boulder marking Sidi Chamarouch

Mule on the trail to the Toubkal Refuge

the square. Follow this out of the village, where the track turns R, then back L. Where it makes a second sharp turn R by a pink house take the footpath that leads straight on.

Continue along the path through fields to a watercourse, passing a house on L. Stay in this line for 100m or so beyond the house until the path starts to switchback. Go up this to reach the motorable dirt road to Aroumd. Take this, past the Cafe Lac d'Ifni (a new building opposite the main village of Aroumd).

Stay on this track, which enters the broad valley base ahead (40mins). It leads to the head of the field system, where an obvious track heads L up the valley side, passing a huge boulder and a few walnut trees. Go past these to where the track levels out a little. It leads in about 2¹/₂hrs to a ford in the stream just below a large white-painted boulder. The boulder marks the shrine, or *marabout*, of Sidi Chamarouch (2340m) and contains a small mosque. It is a popular place of local pilgrimage, as the source which emerges from the rocks here is reputed to have healing powers. The waters are meant to be especially good in curing leg ailments. How true it is

I don't know, but I have seen someone being helped unsteadily down from here by his two friends. When I asked about this, his friends told me that he had been carried up there as a cripple, but now, after three days, he was able to walk.

Across the stream from the shrine, and reached by a small footbridge, is a collection of small shops selling trinkets, chocolate and the ubiquitous tins of sardines. Prices here are some of the most extortionate I've encountered in Morocco.

From Sidi Chamarouch take the steep zigzags on the RH side (true L bank) to emerge onto an easy-angled path leading up the valley. Toubkal is the huge bulk on the opposite bank. An hour or so after Sidi Chamarouch the Tadat pinnacle appears conspicuously on the skyline ahead. The Toubkal hut eventually emerges into view, 20 mins before arrival there (4¹/₂hrs from Imlil).

Lepiney Refuge (3000m)

Remotely situated in the upper Azzaden valley, this is a small hut which receives few visitors. It is delightfully situated near a waterfall. The view outside the hut is

Sidi Chamarouch

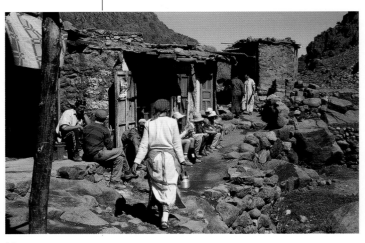

The new Refuge du Toubkal

completely dominated by the cliffs of the Tazaghart plateau, which at 650m are the biggest in the area. At night the lights of Marrakech can be seen. The hut sleeps 20 and has gas stoves but few cooking utensils – take pans and other items. Snow conditions may make the refuge difficult to reach in winter, and in summer it is kept locked when unoccupied. The guardian lives in the first large village down the valley, Tizi Oussem. If travelling to the hut with muleteers make sure they alert the guardian by sending someone ahead. If backpacking there is little alternative to making the detour via Tizi Oussem to fetch the warden. This may explain why it is so rarely visited! It is best to check at the Bureau des Guides in Imlil on how to pick up the key. A new mule track from the Aroumd plain over the pass between Adrar Adj and Aguelzim (Tizi-n-Tizikert) gives quicker access, but can be impassible in winter.

Imlil to Lepiney Refuge

Time:	7–8hrs
Ascent:	1500m
Grade:	strenuous

An early start is advisable. From Imlil, head up the main track from the square. After 250m take a path on the R which heads towards a collection of houses. Pass these and continue heading up the valley towards the Tizi Mzik. A steep mule trail leads in 1½hrs to the col (2485m). (This point can be reached from Aroumd by following the motor road back towards Imlil as far as the first hairpin. A faint track leads off across the L hillside to join up with the main mule trail a few hundred metres below the col.)

From here take the path which contours L across the hillside. After a while the village of Tizi Oussem comes into view below. Where the path appears to split, crossing a steep patch of scree, take the lower junction. Shortly after this the path becomes indistinct while passing through juniper trees. Don't worry if you seem to be losing too much height. The path bends L to skirt a broad gully (the path down to the valley floor is now obvious). Keep contouring and soon the tongue of debris on which Azib Tamsoult is built appears, followed by the *azib* itself. Cross the stream – a good lunch spot (3hrs from Imlil).

From the stream head up L and enter the *azib* on its LH side. This is a good example of a Berber *azib*, utilising the available rocks with fences constructed of massive branches. The tin wreckage is the remains of a one-time climbing club's hut, abandoned in the 1960s.

Continue up through the village to the main riverbed above. The path becomes indistinct again here as it winds its way across frequently wet ground towards the narrows ahead. Cross to the L bank, where a good mule track leads in zig-zags up past some beautiful waterfalls to emerge into a high basin ahead. Continue along the mule track until the refuge is reached (7–8 hours from Imlil).

For **Tacheddirt** and **Oukaimeden refuges**, see main text, above, for access.

EXCURSIONS FROM THE TOUBKAL REFUGE

Toubkal and most of the other highest peaks of the Atlas encircle the head of this valley. All can be done in a day from the hut.

The long screes on the ascent of Jebel Toubkal

Jebel Toubkal (4167m)

This is the highest mountain in North Africa, and the goal of countless visitors who would never normally go near a mountain. Some who make the ascent hate it; I love it. True, the screes are interminable, but at least they are reasonably firm underfoot. Toubkal has several satellite peaks which are described later. The bulk of ascents of Toubkal are made via the S cwm route, which starts directly behind the Toubkal refuge.

Toubkal via S Cwm

Time:	3³⁄₄–5³⁄₄hrs (round trip)
Ascent:	960m
Grade:	strenuous
Warning:	early season snow

From the Toubkal refuge take the path past the rain gauge (with helpful sign on it!) for 50m or so, to where a path leads L to drop down to the river. Cross the river and scramble up the other banks to a good track which leads to the foot of the first screes. Starting from the RH side cross diagonally to boulders and bedrock. From here head up the bed of the cwm on boulders and a scree-covered path to large boulders seen on the skyline from the hut (1hr).

Continue on a well-defined path into the main cwm. There are two alternatives here: L and up a horrible long

63

scree slope to north side of the summit or, much better, head R up steep scree then easier-angled scree leading to the Tizi-n'Toubkal (3940m, 2¼hrs). From here follow the ridge and the path just below the ridge to arrive at the summit (3¼hrs).

The summit is adorned with a large pyramidal iron structure. There are excellent views, heat haze permitting, of distant ranges and peaks: to the south Jebel Sirwa; to the south-east Jebel Sahro. (The nearby conical red peak to the south-east connected to Toubkal is the Dome d'Ifni, or Ouimlilene (3876m), not really feasible from Toubkal.) The small stone shelters on the summit of Toubkal are for bivvying, if you have a good sleeping bag (well worthwhile to enjoy the dawn).

Descend by the same route, which will take between 1½hrs and 2½hrs depending upon your ability and aptitude for scree running.

Toubkal via N Cwm

Time:	4–6hrs
Ascent:	1000m
Grade:	strenuous
Warning:	early season snow

This is the next big cwm down the valley from the refuge. The scree is not as bad as on the normal route. This makes a good combination with the S cwm route.

From the refuge follow the trail down towards Sidi Chamarouch for a few hundred metres, then cross the river before the N cwm entrance. There is a faint track which leads diagonally across the lower scree into the cwm proper. Head up on R of the cwm bed to enter this shortly before it bends round and steepens. Ascend the rock steps which lead to a gap on the L, go up this and continue R towards the main ridge at a col. Follow this to reach the summit (3½hrs–4hrs).

Toubkal via Ouanoums Ridge

Time:	8–9hrs
Ascent:	1000m
Grade:	strenuous
Warning:	climbing, involving abseil

This classic route involves some climbing and is unsuitable for walkers. It is equivalent to alpine grade AD, and is described here for those who feel capable of tackling it.

From the Toubkal (Neltner) refuge take the main path leading up the valley. The col straight ahead is Tizi n'Ouagane; Tizi-n'Ouanoums is the only weakness in the mountain wall to your left (east). After about 45mins reach a stony plain dotted with large boulders. At the

Waterfall on the southern side of the Tizi-n'Ouanoums

65

end of this plain cross the river, then head up the screes on a zigzag path, initially faint, then well engineered, to reach the obvious gap – the Tizi-n'Ouanoums (3664m, 1½hrs–2hrs).

From the col, scramble up the scree to the base of the crag proper. Climb this to reach a chimney which skirts a large pinnacle on the R. This leads to the ridge crest, which is followed to a small col. Climb the face above, trending R, to reach a scree slope. Abseil down into the gap ahead. Ascend the crack (or more easily, go L to reach a loose gully) to arrive on the crest. Follow this to the final real obstacle, a wall which is ascended via a chimney to reach an easier ridge. This leads to a shoulder. Continue along the ridge, much easier now, to a large, rocky eminence (4020m) just before the Tizi-n'Toubkal (4hrs from Tizi-n'Ouanoums). Continue via the normal route to the summit (6hrs–6½hrs).

Satellite Peaks of Toubkal
Tibherine (4010m)
Tibherine can be combined with an ascent of Toubkal via the N cwm, which Tibherine dominates. Head to the col leading to Toubkal and ascend over rocks to the summit, which has the remains of an aircraft which crashed when flying arms to the civil war in Biafra.

Imousser (3890m)
Imousser is just as close. From the col on the main ridge leading up to the Toubkal summit, climb easily up the ridge opposite. At the breach in the ridge drop down to the L to regain the ridge beyond the difficulties. Continue along this, airily, to the summit (25–30mins).

Ouanoukrim (4088m)
A superb mountain, the second highest in the Atlas and one of the most enjoyable – not to be missed. It consists of two summits: the N summit (4083m), known as Ras, and the slightly higher S summit, Timesguida (4088m). The two tops are separated by an easy scree field.

Ouanoukrim via E Ridge

Time:	5½–6hrs
Ascent:	950m
Grade:	strenuous
Warning:	care needed with route finding above the Tizi-n'Ouagane

The normal ascent route, this takes the short ridge descending to the Tizi-n'Ouagane.

From the Toubkal refuge follow the path as for Tizi-n'Ouanoums to where it crosses the stream at the end of the plain (45–50mins). Instead of crossing keep on the R side of the stream and walk up a stony track (steeply at first). This leads into a higher basin (1hr 5mins) that has snow patches even in late summer. The Tizi-n'Ouagane lies straight ahead.

The next section, up to the col, is steep and tiring. In ascent it is probably best to take the RH side, crossing the stream coming in from the R, up to the bedrock. Walk diagonally across, travel over a boulder field low down and rejoin the main path to col (2hrs).

Up from the col the route takes the crested ridge. Skirt the R side of the prominent 7m twin fangs of rock (10mins from the col). Head straight up the crest of the rock ridge (easier than it looks) to reach a track after 70m or so. Head R into a gully and walk up a short way to rejoin the crest, which you follow for a few feet. The angle soon starts to relent until you find yourself on an easy-angled scree slope, the summit scree field (40mins; 2hrs 40mins from the refuge). On the previous section the secret is to keep R of the main crest if in doubt at any stage. **Note:** Make a note of the exit point onto the summit scree field for descending; it is not that easy to find if there are no cairns.

Continue just L of the crest on the R overlooking Akioud, then up screes to reach the summit of the N peak, Ras (4083m, 3hrs). There are fine views of the Toubkal massif. From here it is 20–25mins to the S summit. On descent from the S summit aim for Angour initially (north-east) and avoid dropping down too far R. Rejoin the ascent route just above rock bands. The descent is 50mins to the col and 2hrs–2½hrs back to the refuge.

Ouanoukrim via NW Ridge

Time:	5½–6hrs
Ascent:	950m
Grade:	strenuous
Warning:	easy scrambling

This is not as enjoyable as the normal ascent (there is a lot of scree), although the two can be combined. Proceed as for the normal route as far as the higher basin (1hr 5mins). Head into the obvious side-valley, across some unpleasant ground, to reach the col ahead (Tizi-n'Bou Imrhaz, 3875m, 2½hrs–3hrs).

From here, follow the ridge directly to the N summit. The route is loose in places, but with easy scrambling (1hr from the col; 3½hrs–4hrs in total).

Bou Ouzzal (3860m)

This buttressed ridge between the Tizi-n'Ouanoums and the Tizi-n'Ouagane makes a short but worthwhile expedition in its own right or combined with an ascent of Ouanoukrim.

There are four tops, each of which can be reached with varying degrees of difficulty. The ridge direct involves climbing, but difficulties can be avoided by scrambling detours. The name strictly belongs to the ridge running south with a large plateau of character, which is well worth a visit.

Akioud (4010m)

A fine rocky peak which presents another worthwhile objective from the Toubkal refuge. It is the next peak north from Ouanoukrim, the two being separated by the Tizi-n'Bou Imrhaz.

There are two commonly used routes, but only one easy route for walkers (via the NNW ridge).

Akioud via NNW Ridge

Time:	6hrs
Ascent:	880m
Grade:	strenuous

From the Toubkal refuge a very prominent, deep valley descends to the R of Akioud. The first part of the route tackles this.

From the refuge proceed as for the Tizi-n'Ouanoums route until the level plain just beyond the low yellow crags is reached (40–45mins). Then head R up into the valley, and continue to reach the col. This is the Tizi-n'Amrharas n'Iglioua (3815m, 2½hrs–3hrs), a popular route over to Tazaghart and the Lepiney refuge.

From the col skirt R (westwards) to avoid a rock step, then continue easily to the N summit (40mins from the col). This is the highest of the three main tops of Akioud. Descend via the same route.

Akioud from the Tizi-n'Bou Imrhaz

Time:	6–7½hrs
Ascent:	880m
Grade:	strenuous
Warning:	scrambling

A tiring route over loose scree, its sole merit is in providing a means of traversing Akioud and Ouanoukrim.

Follow the Ouanoukrim NW ridge route as far as the Tizi-n'Bou Imrhaz (2½hrs–3hrs). From here skirt round the base of the wall on the R (east) side and cross the steep scree leading to the col between Akioud and Tadaft. At the col ascend the gully on the R (loose and unpleasant) to emerge on the main Akioud ridge (between the middle top and the higher N summit).

69

Scramble on good rock to the N summit (1½hrs–1¾hrs from col; 4hrs–5½hrs total).

Tadaft (c.3905m)

This is an impressive and much sought-after pinnacle situated on a ridge running from Akioud toward the Mizane valley. Unfortunately it is the area's equivalent of the 'Inaccessible Pinnacle', and beyond the scope of walkers.

Afella (4015m)

Time:	6–6½hrs
Ascent:	890m
Grade:	strenuous

Another popular summit, best reached from the Tizi Melloul. The summit consists of two tops separated by a broad saddle.

From the refuge proceed as for Akioud normal route to the Tizi-n'Amrharas N'Iglioua (3815m, 2½hrs–3hrs). Descend the far side for a short distance until it is possible to traverse R and round the flank and the Tizi Melloul comes into view. Make for the Tizi Melloul, or the broad spur above it on the R. From Tizi Melloul, Afella is a short ascent following the broad spur south-east (20–25mins from Tizi Melloul; 3¾hrs– 4¼hrs total).

Tazaghart Plateau (3984m)

Time:	6–6½hrs
Ascent:	880m
Grade:	strenuous

This huge, weird plateau dominates the west side of the Toubkal area. It is linked by the Tizi Melloul to the other mountains in the range. On the top it is flat enough to land an aircraft. The summit plateau extends for many acres, a stony, desolate place devoid of vegetation. There is little to see up here, but the extraordinary nature of the place makes it an unforgettable experience. There is a shrine somewhere on the plateau which dates back centuries, but I have yet to find it. It is one of the least frequented of the peaks in this region.

From Tizi Melloul follow the easy stepped ridge, scree and path (faint in places) to the edge of the summit

The 'neve permanent' beneath the Tazaghart plateau

The bleak top of the Tazaghart plateau

plateau. The cairn ahead marks the highest point (20–25mins from the col). For an ascent from the Lepiney refuge see Circuit of the Toubkal Region Day 2.

Biguinoussene (3990m)

Time:	5½–6hrs
Ascent:	880m
Grade:	strenuous
Warning:	easy scrambling

North of Afella the bounding ridge of the upper Mizane valley continues as a jagged crest. As a whole it is known as Biguinoussene.

The highest point of this ridge is towards the northern end; the southern pinnacles of the ridge are known as the Clochetons ('bells').

Biguinoussene from Tizi-n'Tadat

Outside the Toubkal refuge a mule track leads straight out from the door towards the screes on the western side of the valley, then traverses across the hillside. Follow this (15mins) to where it arrives at a big gully/rift which leads right up to the main ridge. Walk up the gully bed until it becomes a scramble. Then head out of the bed up steep rock and scree slopes. These lead after about an hour to a horizontal track, well defined. (This is the descent route described as an alternative from Lepiney refuge to Toubkal Refuge (A Circuit of the Toubkal Region, Variations, From the Lepiney refuge)).

Follow the track back towards the gully, below a low rockface. Gain a well-constructed track which leads up to the base of the main scree run, then up to the Tizi-n'Tadat. Fight your way up this (utter misery guaranteed) to reach an abrupt saddle, the Tizi-n'Tadat (c.3725m, 2½hrs). The prominent pinnacle is **Tadat** (c.3755m). The easiest route of ascent is on the shorter south side (UK V Diff. grade, 15m).

Skirt round the base of (or ascend) Tadat and follow the crest of the ridge, without difficulty, to the summit (40mins; 3hrs 10mins from hut).

Continuation from Biguinoussene (The Clochetons)

This involves difficult scrambling/easy climbing in exposed positions. A rope is useful, particularly if an *integrale* ascent is made.

From the summit of Biguinoussene continue along the crest until it begins to dip steeply. Climb down to above a tower. Turn the tower on the R, and continue enjoyably along an exposed crest to reach a *brèche* where the rock ends. Ahead are the Clochetons. Keep on the R side and climb over scree ledges to reach a gap in the Clochetons ridge.

From here a delightful ridge leads to the northern Clocheton: it involves hard scrambling, with some awkward moves. Return along same route to the gap.

From the gap, a horizontal traverse line leads on the R (west) side of the Clochetons to a gap beyond the southernmost Clocheton. Harder variations enable the summits of the Clochetons themselves to be

The alluvial plain above Lac d'Ifni, with Toubkal and satellites on the skyline

attained (3hrs from Biguinoussene; slightly faster in return direction).

Aguelzim (3650m)

This is the continuation ridge north from Tizi-n'Tadat which can be followed as an alternative way back to Imlil instead of the normal Sidi Chamarouch valley route.

From the Tizi-n'Tadat (see preceding walk) follow the ridge, with easy scrambling, to where it overlooks the lower Mizane valley. Continue down to a col – the Tizi-n'Tizikert. From here a path leads down on the R to emerge in the valley above Aroumd. Alternatively keep on the ridge, over Adrar el Hajj (3129m; called Adrar Adj on 1:100,000 maps), to reach the Tizi Mzik (see Circuit of Toubkal Region Day 1). Descend this to Imlil.

The Complete Circuit

It is possible to stay on the ridge crest right the way round from Toubkal to Ouanoukrim, etc, back to Imlil – a fine alpine route. This would take several days. Either bivvy en route or descend to the Toubkal refuge each evening.

For the sake of completeness the traverse should be started by heading L from near Sidi Chamarouch to the Tizi-n'Tarharat, then moving on to Toubkal via Tichki (3627m) and Afekhoi (3751m).

Toubkal from Sidi Chamarouch via Tichki and Afekhoi

Time:	10–12hrs
Ascent:	2000m
Grade:	strenuous
Warning:	scrambling

From Sidi Chamarouch, descend the Imlil track to cross the stream (bridge) and continue for a few minutes until the track starts bending R. Take an indistinct path on the upper side of the track which wends through the crags and angles steeply up into the valley, which leads with effort to the Tizi-n'Tarharat (3456m, 3½hrs). This was the first Atlas feature to be reached by outsiders, in 1871.

Take the N ridge, easy scrambling, which leads to the summit of Tichki (1½hrs from col; **note:** on 1:100,000 map height is given as 3753m). The ridge leads past a series of towers, avoided on either side, to a col, the Tizi-n'Tichki. Continue along the ridge to reach Afekhoi (3751m; 3755m on 1:100,000 maps). The main ridge continues from here to Toubkal.

The section of the circuit most frequently followed from the Toubkal refuge is from Ouanoukrim to Tizi-n'Tadat. This can be done in a long day, returning to the hut. A classic excursion for alpinists.

Ouanoukrim from the summit of Jebel Toubkal

EXCURSIONS FROM THE LEPINEY REFUGE

This is the best base for ascending Tazaghart and Afella, but otherwise there is not a great deal to offer the walker; it is primarily a climber's hut. Tazaghart and Afella are ascended from the Tizi Melloul (see Circuit of the Toubkal Region Day 2 for description of the Lepiney refuge to Tizi Melloul), the approach to which from the Lepiney hut is potentially difficult.

EXCURSIONS FROM TACHEDDIRT

Angour (3616m)

(See Excursions from Oukaimeden, below, for further routes and description.) From Tacheddirt it is possible to scramble directly to the Grouden col and the West ridge, though this is unpleasant and rarely done. A longer but preferable approach is via the Tizi-n'Ouadi. Follow the path above Tacheddirt to Tizi-n'Ouadi (2½hrs, see p.79). From here traverse across north slopes to gain the Grouden col.

Angour via E Ridge

Time:	7½–8hrs
Ascent:	1330m
Grade:	strenuous
Warning:	exposed, easy scrambling

A delightful, airy ridge with a few awkward scrambling sections. From Tacheddirt head up the valley on a prominent mule track (zigzags in the upper part) to the Tizi-n'Tacheddirt (3230m, 2½hrs). At the col ascend directly up the slope to the north via what appears to be a weakness in the rock slabs. Easy scrambling leads to a rocky ridge looking northwards out over the Tissi plateau.

Follow this ridge west, either along the crest itself or just on the RH side, until the last, deepest notch before a rocky slab. Some 5m to the R, down from the col, there is a little rock gully. Go up this for 2m, and traverse R for 30m to easier slabs and scree up to a level, grassy ridge. Head R to the main ridge, and follow this to the lower S summit. The further N summit (3616m) is best climbed from the gap on its RH side via rocky ledges (4½hrs–5hrs). The descent is 3hrs.

Annrhemer (3892m)
A challenging peak with no easy routes; all involve scrambling at the very least. The only route feasible for experienced walkers is described below.

Annrhemer W Ridge from Tizi-n'Tacheddirt

Time:	9hrs
Ascent:	1600m
Grade:	strenuous
Warning:	exposed scrambling

Proceed as for Angour E ridge to the Tizi-n'Tacheddirt (2½hrs). Now head south to the rock outcrop. Easy ground to the L leads back to the main ridge. Continue in this line, avoiding rock outcrops on the L, to follow the ridge just L of the crest.

Where this fades, take a parallel ridge to the L which leads to a fang of rock. Now head past this to reach a prominent col, the Tizi-n'Tigourzatine (3680m, 2hrs from Tizi-n'Tacheddirt).

Follow the ridge to the L of the col, on its RH side. This leads up to the slightly lower W summit. The ridge between here and the main summit is superb – airy and interesting. It has been likened to the Cuillin ridge. Along its crest are some outcrops of lovely rough red granite, the best rock in the area. The scrambling is quite easy throughout. The main summit is reached after 3½hrs from Tizi-n'Tacheddirt (6hrs total).

Descend by the same route.

Annrhemer via NE Ridge

This route is not for walkers, since it involves some easy climbing. Care is required in finding the easiest route, if undue difficulties are to be avoided. A description is included, as an ascent of this, combined with a descent of the previous route (an easier descent), provides far and away the best traverse of the mountain. As the majority of the route is on the north side of the ridge, there is often a fair amount of snow around, even in mid-summer.

From the Tizi-n'Tacheddirt traverse R (eastwards) beneath the N face of Annrhemer to reach a large gully. Ascend this (unpleasant) to where an obvious big scree fan comes in from the R. Ascend this to gain the ridge proper at a small gap.

From the gap follow the crest to where it abuts against a prominent steep step. This is avoided by dropping down R (north) to reach a slender weakness which leads up to a recess. From here regain the ridge and follow it to a gap. Descend down to the R of the gap to enter the gully just below it. Cross this to gain a rake, which leads airily back up to the crest and over further steep ground to a lessening of angle and difficulty. Continue to the summit, mainly on the R side of the ridge.

Bou Iguenouane (3882m)

Compared with Angour and Annrhemer this mountain is lacking in appeal. The scree is particularly tiresome. The peak is often climbed in winter by skiers, as is the Tizi Likemt.

Bou Iguenouane via WSW Ridge

Time:	7½–8hrs
Ascent:	1500m
Grade:	strenuous

From Tacheddirt descend from the village and climb up to the road on the opposite side of the valley. (This can be reached by following the road right round from Tacheddirt – longer but easier.) From the obvious spring at the start of the irrigation channel a deep valley rises ahead, trending up to the L. Follow it, over solid rocks at first, to encounter looser ground and eventually a long scree ascent to the Tizi Likemt (3540m, 3½hrs).

From the col take the ridge on the L to reach a saddle. The ridge becomes narrower. The pinnacles ahead are avoided by contouring their base on the R (south) side. Rejoin the main ridge at a gap, and follow the rocky crest to the summit (5½hrs total).

Descend by the same route.

Aksoual (3912m) and Tamadot (3842m)

Time:	12hrs
Ascent:	1600m
Grade:	strenuous
Warning:	scrambling; bivouac advisable

These twin summits are separated by another highly enjoyable ridge, with easy scrambling. Unfortunately getting there is not so enjoyable. **Note:** On the 1:100,000 map the peak names are written in the wrong places.

In view of the length of the normal route, described below, it is worth considering a bivouac on the Tizi Likemt. This is especially true for those intending to undertake the continuation to Tamadot.

The ENE Ridge

Proceed as for previous route to Tizi-n'Likemt (3540m, 3½hrs). Follow the ridge on the R, easily, over small knolls to where it narrows. Continue along this ridge to reach a col. The ridge leads, with excursions L to avoid difficulties, to the summit of Aksoual (3hrs from Tizi Likemt; 6½hrs total).

Time permitting, the continuation ridge to Tamadot is a must. From the summit of Aksoual descend the ridge, keeping slightly L (south). Reach a col in about 30mins. From here the pinnacled ridge ahead involves rock-climbing. To avoid this descend to the R, on the north side, and follow a good ledge beneath the pinnacles to reach a point between the two main tops of Tamadot (1hr from Aksoual; similar time in reverse).

Aourirt n'Ouassif (2724m)

As seen from Tacheddirt, this is the shapely conical peak just beyond the Tizi-n'Tamatert. It is a day's walk from Tacheddirt or Imlil and can be done as an addition to the walk between the two.

Take the motor road as far as the Tizi n'Tamatert (2279m, 2hrs). From the col ascend the ridge (steeply) to the false summit – the true summit is further W along the ridge (1½hrs from the col).

EXCURSIONS FROM OUKAIMEDEN

Jbel Oukaimeden (3263m)

Time:	2½–3½hrs
Ascent:	650m
Grade:	moderate

This offers potentially the easiest ascent in the Atlas – there is a chair-lift to the top! However it operates only occasionally in the summer. Despite this unsightly intrusion Jbel Oukaimeden makes an excellent short day, or afternoon, walk and has particularly fine views.

From Chez Ju-Ju take the Tizi-n'Ouadi road (leading to the ski-station) up the valley for 50m. Head across the plain, passing houses, to reach the base of the N ridge proper (20mins). Follow the crest of the ridge, steeply, past an abandoned ski-station to the easing of angle and the summit ski-station (1¾hrs). Angour is seen clearly from here, and there is a fine view of the Toubkal range to the south.

Angour (3616m)

A magnificent mountain, one of the finest in the Atlas. It dominates the view SE from Oukaimeden. As seen from here the skyline ridge to the R of the summit is the classic west ridge. The Lakeland pioneer Bentley Beetham climbed the South face back in 1927.

The dominant feature of Angour is the large Tissi plateau which forms the eastern half of the mountain. Unlike the Tazaghart plateau it is low enough for the Berbers to graze sheep and goats on.

Climbing the west ridge, or the easier N gully route, from Oukaimeden involves scrambling. They are not, therefore, suitable routes for the inexperienced.

For other routes on Angour see 'Excusions from Tacheddirt'.

Angour via W Ridge

Time:	6½–7hrs
Ascent:	1000m
Grade:	strenuous
Warning:	exposed scrambling

From Chez Ju-Ju take the Tizi-n'Ouadi road as far as the roadhead. Where the main path heads off, up the side of the valley, continue straight along the valley floor. Ahead and slightly L is an obvious col on the skyline. This is sometimes known as the Grouden col (3090m). There is no real track up to this col, but ascend the R side of the cwm, keeping well to the R to avoid rock outcrops. Arrive at col (1hr 20mins).

From the col the ridge is initially broad. Go along it, keeping to the L of the craggy section, to arrive below the sharp crest of the ridge. Follow the obvious grassy ledges to a flat ledge beneath a crag. Skirt this by going R and scrambling up a weakness to regain the ridge crest. Take the easiest line along this ridge, to where it broadens, and continue to a notch. Ascend the chimney a short way until it is possible to move L on easier ground which leads to a rocky slope. From here pass a step on the R and continue along the ridge crest. This is very narrow and exhilarating, but most of the difficulties can be avoided by detours L or R.

At the end of the ridge drop down a short way to a saddle. Head L to gain the edge of the summit plateau. Continue to arrive at the lower S summit. The main N summit is reached by descending into the gap and climbing up across rock ledges to gain the top (3616m; 4hrs–4½hrs from Oukaimeden).

To descend either return by the same route or reverse the N gully route (quicker but not as pleasant).

Angour via N Gully

Time:	6–6½hrs
Ascent:	1000m
Grade:	strenuous
Warning:	exposed scrambling

While constituting the easiest means of ascent from Oukaimeden, this route nevertheless contains some exposed passages and steep scrambling.

From Chez Ju-Ju take the Tizi-n'Ouadi road, as for the previous route, to the roadhead (45mins). From Angour's impressive N buttress an obvious col can be seen at the base. This is the Tizi-n'Itbir (3288m), clearly marked on maps). To reach this follow the valley which leads towards it. Take the zig-zag track to the col (1½hrs).

Go up the scree to the open gully on the R of the N buttress. Ascend this, taking the easiest line (skirt rock pitches on the R). Continue up the gully bed until a breach in the main buttress can be seen to the L. Aim for this. At the gap an exciting path takes the horizontal ledge across the face – an easy path with terrific views, which leads into another gully that demarcates the N buttress on its eastern side. It can be reached from below (tiring; not recommended). Ascend this easily to the summit plateau. From the gap ascend the N summit as for the previous route (4hrs).

Descend by the same route.

Other Points of Interest in Oukaimeden
A walk up to the radio mast and observation platform gives good views (20mins).

Oukaimeden is famous for its prehistoric rock-carvings. These include daggers, shields and halberds scattered among the village rocks, a remarkable bull overlooking the reservoir, a gem of a hyena across the dam and a frieze of elephants further off. Anyone seriously interested in finding these carvings (not easy) can buy the illustrated guide *Gravures repestres du Haut Atlas*, which covers Yagour and other sites as well.

A CIRCUIT OF THE TOUBKAL REGION
This circuit, designed to be fitted into a two-week holiday, takes in most of the highlights of the region. Numerous variations are possible.

Day 1 Imlil –Lepiney Refuge
From Imlil follow the route over the Tizi Mzik to the Lepiney refuge (3000m) (see Mountain Refuges, Lepiney Refuge, above) (6–7hrs).

Day 2 Lepiney Refuge via Tizi Melloul to Toubkal Refuge

Time:	6½–7hrs
Ascent:	1000m
Grade:	strenuous
Warning:	crosses permanent snow patch – care required

A fine day's walking through outstanding mountain landscape. There is the option of ascending Afella or the Tazaghart plateau.

From the refuge take the path leading up the valley on the L side of the stream-bed past the waterfall. Cross the stream 100m beyond (ill defined). Head over rough ground and make for the toe of a prominent snow-field (marked *neve permanent* on map).

The next section presents the greatest problems on the ascent (and in reverse) with awkward, though solid, scrambling – harder if wet. A rope might be useful as a handrail/security.

Scramble up the gully bed, keeping to the L of the stream, to arrive at the lower rim of a huge cwm (1hr 40mins). The cwm curves round to the R to Tizi Melloul (out of sight). Straight ahead are the Clochetons, with a couple of huge, prominent caves just above the scree at their base.

Follow the bed of the cwm easily to where it turns R and steepens. Tizi Melloul is straight ahead. Expect snowpatches even in autumn. Take the easiest line (mainly on R) up boulders to the col. Arrive slightly R of the lowest point of the col, skirting snowpatches (3875m, 3¼hrs).

Tazaghart (see Excursions from Toubkal Refuge, Tazaghart Plateau) is an easy ascent from this col. Follow the easy stepped ridge R (scree and a faint path in places) to arrive on the edge of the plateau. The prominent cairn just ahead marks the highest point (3970m; 20mins from the col). Descend by the same route to the col (15–20mins).

Afella (4015m) is a slightly longer alternative from the col. Follow the obvious broad ridge to the E to arrive at a saddle between the two tops – the N top is slightly higher (30–35mins from the col).

At the col the route skirts round the prominent spur of Afella ahead on the L (the ascent of Afella from the Toubkal refuge in reverse – see Excursions from Toubkal Refuge, Afella). Contour round to the L, descending slightly, to turn this spur and ascend to the Tizi-n'Amrharas n'Iglioua (see Excursions from

Toubkal Refuge, Akioud via NNW Ridge), 1½hrs from Tizi Melloul.

Drop down the screes on the other side, keeping to the R side of the deep valley, to emerge in the upper Mizane valley at the level plain before the Tizi-n'Ouanoums turn-off. Follow the main path down to the Toubkal refuge (3½hrs from Tizi Melloul; 6¾hrs from Lepiney refuge).

Day 3 Toubkal Refuge

An opportunity to ascend Toubkal or one of the other peaks here (see Excursions from the Toubkal Refuge, above).

Day 4 Toubkal Refuge via Tizi-n'Ouanoums to Lac d'Ifni

Time:	5–6hrs
Ascent:	450m
Grade:	strenuous
Warning:	snow in early season

Take the good path from the hut which heads up the valley. Stay on the R bank of the stream. After 30mins pass beneath yellow crags on the R (the path is a little indistinct here). The Tizi-n'Ouanoums is the next prominent notch in the L valley wall after Toubkal S cwm.

The path soon becomes clear again as it winds its way through rock outcrops. After 45mins reach a stony plain dotted with several large boulders. Cross this to its end, then cross the river. (The path to Tizi n'Ouagane and Ouanoukrim carries on along the R bank here.) Work your way up the scree slopes, initially on a faint track, then on a well-engineered zigzag track, to reach the col abruptly (3664m, 1½hrs–2hrs). The lake is visible from here, though it later disappears from view. Note that the ascent from the Toubkal Refuge side can often be covered in steep snow until mid-summer; an ice-axe is advisable in early season.

The descent from the col to Lac d'Ifni is one of the longest in the Atlas, being fully 1500m (5000ft). Fortunately it is on a reasonable path, though this can often be faint or eroded in the early season. Descend this path, which is through impressive rock scenery, to enter an area of huge boulders. The path winds its way through these to emerge onto a desolate alluvial plain. The lake is 30mins further on. Aim for the L bank (north side) of the lake. Following this path round you find a campsite, with a few dry-stone walls for shelter, slightly beyond half-way down the lake.

Seen at close quarters the scummy appearance of the lake does not serve to make it inviting. However, I

The summit col of Tizi-n'Ouanoums, looking towards the Dome d'Ifni

know plenty of people who have swum here with no ill effects. Besides, the lake is the only source of drinking water!

The bands around the water's edge are the result of attempts to regulate the inflow. The lake – the only one in the Toubkal ranges – is stocked with trout.

For all its proximity to the lake the campsite is still a bleak place, and very exposed to the wind. You may wish to continue for another hour or so to Imhilene, the first of the villages in the Tifnoute valley below (see next day's route notes).

The rocky approach to Lac d'Ifni

Day 5 Lac d'Ifni via Amsouzart to Tissaldai

Time:	6–7hrs
Ascent:	400m
Grade:	moderate

Continue from the campsite to reach the end of the lake. As the path climbs you realise that the Lac d'Ifni is a lake without any outflow. At the top of the rise the path follows the edge of the steep valley side. The mounds which block the eastern end of the lake are probably not glacial in origin, but fluvial.

Descend into the Tifnoute valley and the first village, Imhilene, and continue past walnut groves down the valley. There is a choice of paths on either side of the valley. Both lead to Amsouzart (see Toubkal Region, Peripheral Bases, Southern Approaches), where there are several shops. There is even one shop with a fridge here. The road has brought electricity with it, and you can telephone here in case of emergency.

From Amsouzart another valley leads north into the mountains. This is the Tissaldai valley (or Assif n'Tisgui), and it provides a delightful walk for the next part of the route. It is very fertile and in autumn there is plenty of fresh fruit to be had. Take the path which leads north from Amsouzart, on the RH side of the valley initially. At the narrows just beyond Timzakine keep on the R bank and pass through Tagadirt. Skirt round the spur ahead, and at a junction in the path take the lower route. This leads to Missour and, shortly, to Tissaldai (2100m; 6–7hrs from Lac d'Ifni). There is a good campsite under walnut trees opposite the village.

Day 6 Tissaldai via Tizi-n'Terhaline to Azib Tamenzift

Option 1	
Time:	7½hrs
Ascent:	1550m
Grade:	strenuous

Option 2	
Time:	8hrs
Ascent:	1300m
Grade:	strenuous

Beyond the village the valley turns west and becomes narrower. Follow the track, which leads to an upland basin. Follow the stream then climb up a gully to the R of a knoll. The path to the L leads eventually to the same point, but is longer.

Emerge on top of the knoll. There is a small *azib* on the L, Irhir-n'Tarbaloute (2630m). The track now starts to ascend the valley head, easily at first then directly up the hillside on the R via a series of zigzags.

Gain the col, which is a smooth saddle on the ridge. This is the Tizi-n'Terhaline (3350m; called Tizi-n'Ounrar Imaghka on 1:100,000 maps). Ahead lies the upper Tifni basin, a high and remote area which drains into the upper Ourika valley.

The path which leads off to the L arrives eventually at the broad saddle of the Tizi-n'Tarharat. Don't take this, but drop straight down without undue difficulty into a valley which emerges at Azib Tifni (2820m). This is another good example of a Berber *azib*; there isn't a building here over a metre in height.

From Azib Tifni there are two alternative routes.

Option 1: Head back up the valley on the L for a short distance to the head of the cultivated section. From here head up the hillside in an easterly direction to reach the Tizi-n'Tifourhate (*c.*3130m). Descend to Azib Amtou, the first village beyond the gorge (1¾hrs from Azib Tifni; 3¾hrs from the col).

Option 2: Follow the track through the gorge, after an initial scramble, crossing the river several times to emerge below Azib Amtou. This is the longer route, but it has less ascent and more interest. Continue along the L side of the valley to cross the river to Azib Tamenzift, the only village on the R bank. There is a good bivvy site next to the path by some large boulders 200m beyond the village. (**Warning:** kitbags have been stolen from here in the past.)

Day 7 Azib Tamenzift via Tizi Likemt to Tacheddirt

Time:	6hrs
Ascent:	1050m
Grade:	strenuous

From the bivvy site cross the river and follow the track diagonally up the hillside (E). This skirts the top of Azib Likemt, another summer residence where the highest building is no more than a metre high (20mins).

Continue N up the steep side-valley on a good track, staying high to the L of the valley bed. The path leads (without shade) in 3hrs to the col, the Tizi Likemt (3555m), crossing scree for the last 400m.

Look down the other side into the Imenane valley and be thankful that the pass is being ascended in this direction! Below lie some of the longest scree slopes you are likely to encounter in the region. The scree in the upper third is superb for running down (and horrible to ascend). Beyond this the scree becomes harder and less mobile. The route is painfully obvious, and leads straight down to the dirt road and a welcome spring. Camping here is popular, but beware scorpions.

Those staying in the Tacheddirt CAF refuge should head straight down from the road, passing terraces, to the river and ascend directly to Tacheddirt. Alternatively there is a good bivvy site reached by taking the dirt road R along the hillside. Pass boulders blocking the track and continue along until just before the road crosses the main riverbed above Tacheddirt. The bivvy site is amongst large boulders just above a little gorge to the L. Beware of scorpions.

From the col, it is possible to ascend Bou Iguenouane (3882m; see Excursions from Tacheddirt) via the WSW ridge (3½hrs–4hrs return to col).

Day 8 Tacheddirt via Tizi-n'Tacheddirt to Ourika valley

Time:	6¾hrs
Ascent:	940m
Grade:	strenuous

This day takes you into the remote upper Ourika valley. From Tacheddirt follow the well-defined track up the valley to the Tizi-n'Tacheddirt (3230m, 2½hrs; see Excursions from Tacheddirt). At the col descend the well-defined track, following the L side of valley, to drop down zig-zags and arrive below some rocky outcrops. There is water hereabouts on the R. Keep descending. After about 1½hrs from the col a well-made path contours off to the L – don't take this. The village of Labassene (c.2240m) comes into view, high above the narrow valley floor. Take the higher path at the junction to enter above the village (2¼hrs from the col; 4¾hrs total).

Walk through the village to reach a well-made horizontal track, and follow this to zigzags down to the

The upper Ourika valley

river (35mins from village; 2hrs 50mins from the col). The path contours above the river again. Suddenly the main Ourika valley comes dramatically into view: Timichchi is the village straight across on the opposite side of the valley; in the foreground is the small hamlet of Aguerd n'Ourtane. Take the higher path at the bifurcation just ahead, then drop straight down to Timichchi (1850m; 4¼hrs from the col, 6¾hrs from Tacheddirt).

There is a village house in Timichchi belonging to the headman where food and accommodation are available. The refuge marked on 1:50,000 map is an old CAF hut, no longer in existence. For camping continue further up the Agounns valley to walnut groves. During the summer months it may be necessary to walk a kilometre or so before running water is encountered.

Day 9 involves a long ascent; in summer parties may therefore wish to continue as far as Agounss, avoiding the worst of the heat with an early start.

Day 9 Timichchi via Tizi-n'Ouhattar to Oukaimeden

Time:	6½hrs
Ascent:	1300m
Grade:	strenuous

This day involves a very long toil over the Tizi-n'Ouhattar, another of the great Atlas passes and a masterpiece of route finding. Due to the relatively low altitude from which this route starts, an early start pays dividends during the summer months.

From Timichchi cross the riverbed to the L bank and follow the track (on the opposite side of valley to that shown on the 1:50,000 map) and the riverbed. About 400m past Ait Chao, where the valley turns to the L, cross to the R bank and head steeply up what at first appears to be a dry gully bed (25–30mins). Emerge onto a track leading to Animiter. There are impressive views of the N summit of Angour.

Continue through Tinoummer to Agounss, a large straggling village at the head of the valley (1hr 5mins). Immediately on arrival, head back R up a zigzag dirt track to enter the upper part of the village beneath the mosque. This is unmistakeable with its new concrete minaret. Pass beneath the mosque, taking the L (horizontal) path (1½hrs) which runs up through the village onto a stony path leading to the col. Stay well to the R of the large, solitary tree. This is a long, hot slog without any shade, water or vegetation.

An abrupt finish brings you to the col (3140m, 4½hrs) and a dramatic contrast in scenery: ahead lies the grassy basin of Oukaimeden with its modern apartment blocks and radio mast.

There is a long descent to Azib Tiferguine (50mins from the col), with a spring just before the *azib*. Continue down the valley and L across the grassy plain to Oukaimeden (2hrs from col; 6hrs 30mins total). Pass the CAF refuge before Chez Ju-Ju.

Day 10 Oukaimeden via Gliz to Amssakrou

Time:	3–3½hrs
Ascent:	150m
Grade:	easy

This and the next day's walk can easily be combined. However, by splitting the walk you have the opportunity to spend a night in Amssakrou, an interesting experience. It also means getting back to Marrakech at a reasonable time on the following day. (**Note:** Amssakrou is written as Amskere on 1:50,000 maps.)

From Chez Ju-Ju follow the road up to the col (Tizi-n'Oukaimeden 2682m), passing modern houses (15mins). Drop down the RH side of the col on a good track. Ahead in the near distance is an obvious wooded red-earth ridge with a new dirt road on the R. The village of Agadir is just visible to the L of the ridge, over the

93

saddle. Aim for Agadir, following the path until you are on a broad ridge with many junipers.

Reach a little knoll on the ridge where a path heads off L. Take the path down to fields and towards the villages of Agadir and Imsourene. About 300m before the first village (1hr) the path divides; carry straight on towards Imsourene and Agadir. Take the L fork which leads down the hillside. The path you take after the valley bottom is obvious, heading steeply up to a large grassy platform, then R to the col.

Follow the path down, crossing a new dirt road (which leads to a copper mine) to reach the attractive village of Gliz (1hr 20mins). The narrow, steep main street provides plenty of good photo opportunities. It leads down out of the village to the river. Cross the river and ascend steeply (past a small waterfall) for 20mins to reach the grassy platform at the RH end (1hr 55mins).

A further 20mins' easy walking along a mainly level path leads to the col (c.2210m, 2¼hrs). There are good views ahead of the Tizi-n'Aguersioual, tomorrow's route. Take a good path down, contouring on the L hillside, and emerge above Amssakrou (50mins from col; 3hrs 5mins total).

Amssakrou is beautifully situated in a bowl surrounded by a fine series of terraces. Either stop in one of the village houses or camp by the river. As you enter the village from the RH side, the first house on the R in the horizontal street ahead takes in trekkers. Step inside this house and you are back in the Middle Ages. Notice the door-lock; it is made entirely of wood, even down to the wooden key. Narrow passageways lead out onto the flat roof of the house below.

Day 11 Amssakrou via Tizi-n'Aguersioual to Imlil

Time:	2½–3hrs
Ascent:	350m
Grade:	easy

Take the path-cum-drainage channel down the RH side of the village and wind your way down through terraces to the river. It is east to get lost here as the multitude of tracks is very confusing. If in doubt just keep heading downhill.

On the opposite bank is a series of newly planted terraces of trees. Aim for the RH side of these, passing a few houses on the way. Once here the path is obvious. Follow it for 45mins to the col (Tizi-n'Aguersioual, c.2030m) and a junction with the main Ikkis track which comes in from the L.

Take the track heading straight down to Aguersioual (1hr 40mins). Walk through the village, which seems relatively affluent after Amssakrou, and at the wide, horizontal track turn L. This leads pleasantly along the valley, soon dropping down to the river. Cross the river to regain the main road which leads in 45mins to Imlil (2hrs 40mins).

Variations
Numerous variations are possible on the route above, depending on time available.

From the Lepiney Refuge
An easier alternative to the Tizi Melloul route is via the Tadat col. A good deal shorter, it nevertheless involves a fair amount of loose, unpleasant scree on the descent. This route is marked (red dotted line) on the 1:50,000 map, and passes by the famous Tadat pinnacle (see Excursions from Toubkal Refuge, Biguinoussene) on the col.

Take the path behind the refuge for a short way up the valley. Up to the L there is a large amount of scree beneath the cliffs. To the R a deep gully descends, not clearly seen from the refuge. When this becomes more apparent aim for the buttress on its L, just above the gully exit. Climb diagonally up the scree (loose, no real path) to gain the rocky ledges on the buttress, well above its toe.

Traverse R easily until the route above becomes clear: it follows the rocky rib just to the L of the gully bed and is cairned in places. Ascend for 30m or so to reach a narrow, grassy ledge with a large quartz-faced boulder on it. Take this ledge to its end, and continue scrambling upwards (no technical difficulty) to where the gully widens into a steep cwm. Aim straight for the headwall above. Here there is a well-defined horizontal path which leads to an obvious gap in the ridge (2¼hrs). The Tadat col can be clearly seen from here (across the other side of the bowl and slightly higher).

Follow the horizontal track, crossing a snow patch half-way. Take care here – this was the scene of a fatal accident a few years ago. Climb the final short gully to arrive at Tadat col just below the pinnacle (c.3720m, 2¾hrs). At the col the view is dominated by Toubkal, directly across the valley. The S cwm route is clearly seen in its entirety. The Toubkal refuge is not, however, visible.

Descend straight down the gully on steep scree, which gives a good run until it peters out. From here trend L to avoid the craggy section below. Soon, improbably, an ancient mule track is encountered. This track dates back to when copper and silver were mined here. Green veins of malachite can be seen everywhere. Take this track, which leads down to arrive at a horizontal traverse below a low crag. Take this L as far as a spur.

The quickest way down from here is to aim for the bed of the main gully below. As you can see it is not a very attractive prospect. The alternative is longer but involves less actual scrambling.

Shops at Sidi Chamarouch

Continue L along the traverse path until an obvious scree gully descends to the valley floor. Cross the head of the gully diagonally to the far side. Descend on the L side of the gully to narrows, avoiding the step, to gain easier grassy ground. Continue in this line until a faint diagonal track leads off R up the valley. Take this to the Toubkal refuge (3207m; 2½hrs from col).

From the Toubkal Refuge

Time:	8–9hrs
Ascent:	1150m
Grade:	strenuous

It is possible to reach Azib Tamenzift in a day, rather than three days as per the route above. This means going via the Tizi-n'Tarharat and omitting Lac d'Ifni. This is, however, a long walk.

From the refuge, descend the valley to Sidi Chamarouch (1¼hrs). Cross the bridge below the village and continue for a few minutes. When the track starts to bend R head up the slope on an indistinct path which angles into the valley leading to the Tizi-n'Tarharat. It heads laboriously up to the pass, the bleak saddle at the summit of the Tizi-n'Tarharat (3456m, 4¾hrs), passing a spring after about 3½hrs.

Take the well-defined path which leads off NE to contour across the hillside. This starts to trend E and leads to a steep spur. Descend this, which takes you to the head of the Azib Tifni pastures, and rejoin the normal route at Azib Tifni (1½hrs from the col).

From Amsouzart

Rather than continuing up the Tissaldai valley it is possible to head directly to Azib Likemt via the Tizi-n'Ourai. As this would be a very long day from Lac d'Ifni, it is best to spend the night in Amsouzart.

Time:	7–8hrs
Ascent:	370m
Grade:	strenuous

Continue up the valley N as far as the next village on the R bank (Timzakine). Scramble up the hillside for a short way above the village to reach a good horizontal track. Follow this south, soon turning east to skirt a spur, then regaining the crest of this spur. Follow the track to a junction and take the L fork, leaving the spur. Continue in this line to gain the obvious col (Tizi-n'Ourai, 3120m; this is called Tizi-n'Ououraine on 1:50,000 maps).

Descend on the track which parallels the stream. After about 500m take the higher path; don't drop down just yet. The main track leads to a confluence of two streams. Cross here and follow the R bank of the stream down to emerge at a bivvy site just beyond Azib Tamenzift (7–8hrs).

From Tacheddirt

Time:	3½hrs
Ascent:	640m
Grade:	moderate

It is possible to walk to Oukaimeden in a short day via the Tizi-n'Ouadi (2928m).

Above Tacheddirt a broad track contours the hillside. Gain it and follow it to its end. Take the continuation track which leads towards a rocky rib. Where the track divides take the lowest path, which soon starts to climb steeply. It leads to a false col, and the true col is 400m further on (1¾hrs).

To descend, take the very obvious track which leads down to the valley and the start of a motor road. Go past the ski-station to arrive in Oukaimeden by Chez Ju-Ju (3½hrs).

OUTLYING SUMMITS

These peaks are too far from the main bases to facilitate an easy ascent: they are included as worthwhile objectives if time permits.

Adrar-n-Dern (3853m)

This large, featureless mound overlooking Amsouzart and the upper Souss valley is of little interest in itself, but provides a useful link with Iferouane.

From Amsouzart head up the Tizgui valley towards Tissaldai. After a few hundred metres a track can be seen on the far spur of the deep valley to the R. Gain this track and follow it to the Tizi-n'Ourai (3109m).

Follow the ridge on the R which leads to the W spur (3528m). Continue without difficulty to the main summit (3853m). Immediately to the north there is a col separating Adrar-n-Dern from Iferouane.

Iferouane (3996m)

Marked as 4001m on the 1:50,000 map, this probably accounts for the majority of ascents. It has, unfortunately, been revised down. The first foreign ascent was made on the peak on the assumption that it was the highest in the Atlas.

This makes a pleasant, if long, ridge walk from Adrar-n-Dern. From there skirt round the cwm to the north to reach a forepeak. Continue along the main ridge to gain the summit. The NW cwms offer fine ski runs.

Adrar Meltsen (3595m)

This distinctive bulk dominates the view down the upper Ourika valley. It can be climbed in a long day from Setti Fadma via the SW ridge (9hrs from Setti Fadma). From the summit it is possible to follow a long crest north-east to the hamlet of Ikis above the lower Zat valley and the dirt track out. A circular traverse from the north is recommended for those visiting Yagour.

Taskka-n-Zat (3912m)

The highest point on the south-bounding ridge of the Toubkal Atlas, Taskka-n-Zat is difficult of access. Lying at the head of the Zat valley it can be reached most easily from the Ourika valley the Tizi-n'Tilst and the upper gorges of the Ouid Zat.

Hamish Brown has done a traverse of this ridge from the Tizi-n'Tagharat via Adrar-n-Dern to Taskka-n-Zat. A fine expedition taking several days (see Bibliography).

Yagour Plateau

A very large plateau to the north-west of Setti Fadma, its principal attraction is the excellent prehistoric rock-carvings to be found on its flanks to the north of Azib Amdouz. The circuit of Yagour, returning by the Tizi-n'Oughre, is a fine two-day walk from Amdouz.

THE MGOUN MASSIF

Although much less frequented by the visitor than the Toubkal region, the Mgoun massif is within relatively easy reach of Marrakech and offers some of the most superlative walking anywhere in Morocco, as well as fabulous local architecture. A visit is well worth the effort.

The Mgoun massif, unlike the Toubkal region, consists of the typical sedimentary rocks of the High Atlas with their characteristic escarpments, long crested ridges (e.g. Tarkeddid) and deep gorges cut by rivers through the softer rocks as the young fold mountains have risen. The summit of the Mgoun massif, variously called Irhil Mgoun or Amsod (4068m), is the highest point in the Atlas outside the Toubkal area.

Described here is a circuit of nine to ten days, which could quite feasibly be accomplished during a two-week holiday. Numerous variations are possible, and several of the days could be combined if time is short. One of the variations is a trip through the Tessaout (Wandras) gorge; this involves an escape pitch (V diff. in standard) for which a rope and slings are needed.

PROVISIONS

The Mgoun area differs from Toubkal in that here you pass through remote, roadless country where the only foods available are occasional eggs, bread and potatoes. In autumn fresh fruit can be found, but in general you need to carry the bulk of your supplies while on trek. Where small shops exist on route they are mentioned in the route notes.

ACCESS

From the north-west the usual point of departure is either Marrakech or Beni Mellal. Take the bus or service taxi to the provincial centre of Azilal. Using the tarred road to the Ait Bougoumez you could, alternatively, hire a taxi from Marrakech; when the taxi is shared with a group, this is a good option.

Azilal is no substitute for Marrakech when it comes to shopping, but all basic foodstuffs required for a trek can be purchased here. There are a few basic cafes and cheap hotels, should you wish to break the journey. Hotel Tanoute is probably the best, with a double room costing 150dh.

Nearby, and the only other reason for staying in Azilal, are the well-known Cascades d'Ouzoud ('falls of the olives'), 30km or so from town. These 100m-high falls drop over buttresses of tufa, and swimming (though banned) is often possible in the pools below. Certainly it is a nice place to relax either before or after a trek.

For onward travel to the Ait Bougoumez valley, the starting point for trekking, there is a (usually crowded) minibus which leaves Azilal at lunchtime, but ask about alternatives that are now beginning to operate. The road to Ait Mohamed is followed, but before that place is reached a new road breaks right and runs through high country before twisting down to run up the Oued Lakdar valley and into the Bougoumez from its lower end, a scenically superb run. The old way in by Ait Mohamed and a pass to the upper end of Bougoumez was rough and often impassible because of snow. The new road offers all-year access and is cleared when snow falls. The tarmac leads to Tabant, the administrative centre of the valley (Sunday souk).

VALLEY BASES (MULE HIRE AND LOCAL GUIDES)

Driving along the broad, flat Ait Bougoumez valley, one cannot help but be struck by the exotic villages that line the road. Multi-storey mud-brick kasbahs exist here in abundance, and make an interesting place in which to stay.

For the circuit described the starting point is the village of Iskattafene, conveniently central. Here one can ask for accommodation in the village and be directed to a suitable *gîte*. It is also a good place to hire mules.

The densely populated nature of the Ait Bougoumez valley means that villages tend to merge into one another – Iskattafene is a half-hour walk from Tabant, the focal point and where transport terminates.

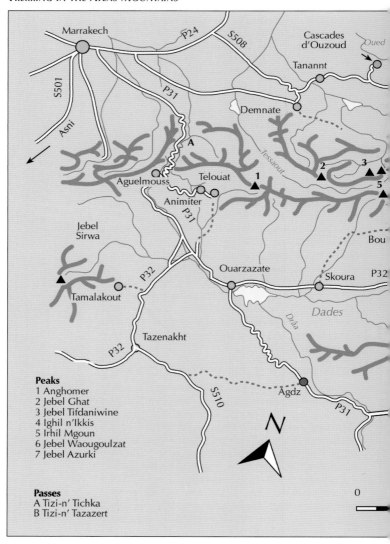

Peaks
1 Anghomer
2 Jebel Ghat
3 Jebel Tifdaniwine
4 Ighil n'Ikkis
5 Irhil Mgoun
6 Jebel Waougoulzat
7 Jebel Azurki

Passes
A Tizi-n' Tichka
B Tizi-n' Tazazert

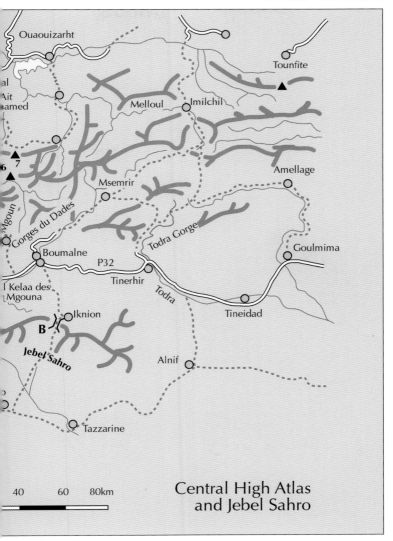

Central High Atlas
and Jebel Sahro

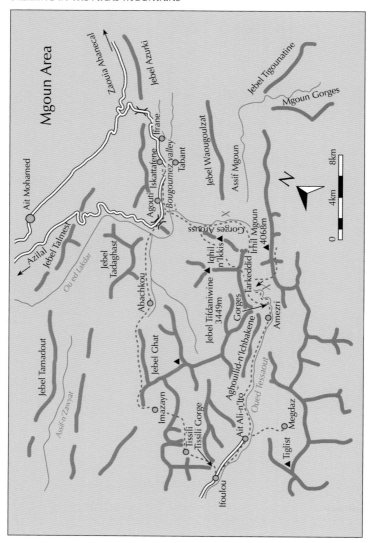

Mgoun Area

Zaouia Ahanecal

Jebel Azurki

Jebel Tigounatine

Mgoun Gorges

Ait Mohamed

Azilal

Jebel Talmest

Tifrane

Agouti Iskattafene

Bougoumez valley

Tabant

Jebel Waougoulzat

Assif Mgoun

Ou ed Lakdar

Jebel Tadaghast

Abachkou

Gorges Arouss

Iqhil n'Ikkis

Irhil Mgoun 4068m

Tarkeddid

Jebel Ghat

Jebel Tifdani'wine 3449m

Gorges

Amezri

Aghoulid-n-I'chbakene

Jebel Tamadout

Assif-n-Zawyat

Imazayn

Oued Tessaout

Ait Ali-n'Ito

Tissili

Tissili Gorge

Megdaz

Tiglist

Ifoulou

N

0   4km   8km

The Tessaout valley

Tabant has a *teleboutique* and basic shops, and is a good source of both guides and mule hire. There should be qualified guides as well as local guides present – the National Guide Training School is here. There are one or two *gîtes* dotted around the village, offering reasonable accommodation. You may want to consider carrying on to Imelghas (also known as Iskattafene), however, and trying to find a *gîte* of character – no problem, as the bus will continue up-valley. Mohammed Achari owns one *gîte* with character: try the *hammam*.

Atlas Sahara Treks, run by Bernard Fabry, operates several treks both in the Mgoun area and throughout the Atlas. The company maintains an attractive hotel, built in vernacular style, in Ifrane, at the upper end of the valley. The company can be contacted via its office in Marrakech:

Atlas Sahara Treks
72 Rue de la Liberte
Marrakech
Tel: (4) 33757.

TABANT TO ISKATTAFENE

At 2–3km, this is the shortest walk described in the guide! Head out of Tabant on the Azilal road, passing the *teleboutique* and school. Just beyond the bridge over the well-controlled river take the track heading off right along the bank and then across fields. This leads first to the village of Imelghas then to Iskattafene, the next village along, a maximum of 30mins from Tabant.

A CIRCUIT OF THE REGION

Day 1 Iskattafene to Abachkou

Time:	6½hrs
Ascent:	20m
Grade:	moderate

From Iskattafene continue west along the Ait Bougoumez valley (over fields as far as Agouti if wanting to avoid the tarmac), through lush countryside dotted with trees (storks nesting) and rich villages. Follow the main road from Agouti. After a deep cutting a fine view is obtained of the deep Lakhdar valley ahead. Where the road splits take the LH branch which descends to the village of Aguersif. (There is a direct pedestrian/mule path down to Aguersif.)

Continue upstream (south-west) to the large village of Iguelouene, where a couple of shops sell eggs, oil, sardines, etc.

Turn L at the top of the village, to the R side of a large kasbah with a collapsed corner, and continue on a mule track on the RH side of the valley. A strung-out collection of houses forms Abachkou (1800m, 6½hrs, telephone). There is a good campsite by the river at the upper end of the village, beneath walnut trees.

Day 2 Abachkou to Tarbat-n-Tirsal

Time:	6hrs
Ascent:	600m
Grade:	moderate

Head up the valley, passing the village of Ighboula on the R and a light-coloured kasbah up on the L. Walk firstly along a dry riverbed (mid-summer onwards) then on a good mule track (steep at first) up to a col – the Tizi-n-Tighist (2399m, 3hrs). There are some very good prehistoric rock-carvings, showing battle scenes and animals, on sandstone rocks only a few yards from the track.

Continue on the track (well defined) past a spring, on the south side of the valley, opposite the village of Tagassalt. Turn L along the broad, cultivated side valley before the main valley enters a rocky defile. Camp opposite the village (6hrs).

Day 3 Tarbat-n-Tirsal to Imazayn

Time:	7hrs
Ascent:	300m
Grade:	moderate

Follow a mule track in the SW valley below the cliffs of Jebel Ghat (also known as Jebel Rat and Jebel Rhat). Here you may well encounter black kites. Walk up to a col (2850m), skirting a subsidiary spur which runs down from the summit crest. Going around this spur the track fades. Keep on a slightly rising traverse until a further col is reached. There are impressive views from here.

Drop down into the valley, heading west-south-west (steep in places) passing a good possible campsite. Where the path heads L to a saddle, take it L down to Imazayn, and then to Tazaght just below (7hrs). In Imazayn is a shop selling Coke, eggs, and few tinned goods and biscuits. Either stop in the village or cross the valley to camp on an obvious large, flat platform opposite the villages. (There is water by a stone building just up behind the platform on the LH side.)

Jebel Ghat

If time permits, this is a most worthwhile undertaking. The ridge as a whole would be a very long walk, probably taking two days.

From the campsite mentioned above (on descent to Imazayn), reverse the route to the col. The wearying ascent leads straight up from here to Pt.3564. Head west-south-west to the summit (3781m, 5–7hrs). A scree descent from here leads in 3hrs back to the campsite. The route as a whole provides good, non-technical scrambling. The best route is from the high Tizi-n-Iblouzene, south-east of the summit (springs), which also offers access to the higher, if overshadowed, Jebel Tignoust, 3819m.

Day 4 Imazayn/Tazaght via Tissili Gorge to Ifoulou

Time:	6½hrs
Ascent:	200m
Grade:	moderate

From the large grass platform take the path on the RH side. This leads up over shaly ground into a stream-bed (10mins). Follow this small valley upwards, and 30m after crossing a stream take the R bank and continue along a track parallel to the stream-bed (spring over to the L after 35mins).

Quit the stream bottom after ¼ mile for the grassy ridge on the R. Follow the ridge path, mainly on the L side, to an obvious grassy col (1hr, c.2550m). Descend in a southerly direction to an obvious track which follows a rocky spur straight down to a small *azib*. (Avoid the well-defined track contouring the hillside to the L – it leads up into a high valley.)

From the lowest part of the *azib* either:

1) follow the bed of the gorge, impressive and easy walking (but only if river is not in spate)

2) cross the river just below the *azib*, and take a mule track on the L side of the gorge. Again there are fine views, and route-finding is easy; just follow the path which leads obviously towards the end of the gorge.

Both routes arrive at the village of Imi-n-Tizgui. For the last 100m or so into the village, follow an irrigation channel on the RH side of the valley.

From Imi-n-Tizgui continue down the valley (much broader now) to Tissili (*c*.1980m, 3½hrs). This is a large, fairly affluent village with dirt road connections to the Haouz plain. There is at least one shop here which sells bread, eggs, and the usual selection of tinned sardines, biscuits, etc. The Tissili gorge can be seen clearly from this village.

Descend to the river and follow the obvious gorge south (spring ¼ mile after Tissili). This is delightful, easy walking amidst impressive scenery. (In times of spate great care needs to be taken with river crossings here.) Eventually you enter the main Oued Tessaout valley (6½hrs) between the villages of Ifoulou (downstream) and Fakhour.

There is a campsite downstream facing Ifoulou, a pleasant level area of grass on the L bank (and usually a bridge). Mosquitos are a problem here, as they are throughout the Tessaout valley in summer.

Day 5 Ifoulou via Fakhour to Ait Ali-n-Ito

Time:	2¾hrs
Ascent:	100m
Grade:	easy

This is a very short walk, a relief after the last two tiring days. A dirt track follows the river the whole way to Amezri.

Continue up the valley past Fakhour (a fine restored *agadir*) to the next large village – Ait Ali-n-Ito (2¾hrs). Here there is an unexpected *gîte* where you can stay cheaply. As you arrive the *gîte* is the small building facing you at the furthest side of the village – hollyhocks grow outside it. Inside, the house is elaborately decorated, clearly a cut above its neighbours. Its hot showers and *hammam* are most welcome. The guardian will also do a good *tajine* or *cous-cous*, and provides walnuts to eat with the mint tea.

Variation

For those who desire a more active day, take the Tasselnt valley south from Ifoulou (attractive walking) to Tagoukht village, beyond which you head up the side-valley to the east to the Tizi n'Ougharghir, 2454m (not named on the map). The 2766m summit just to the north (J. Azlam) is a

The lower section of the Tessaout gorge

good viewpoint. Descend into more barren country eastwards and take left forks to eventually come down into Megdaz, often described as the most fascinating village in the Atlas – an architectural gem. From there a dirt track runs downvalley to Ait Ali-n-Ito.

Day 6 Ait Ali-n-Ito via Ichbakene to Amezri

Time:	5½hrs
Ascent:	200m
Grade:	moderate

The route follows the river the whole way. Once again crossings are made more difficult by heavy rain, and the route can be difficult in spring. Follow the dirt track, initially on the L side of the valley. Ait Hamza has an interesting watermill beside the path. In 3½hrs reach Ichbakene. (**Note:** The map is wrong here! Ichbakene is wrongly positioned. In fact it is roughly half-way between Amezri and Ait Ali-n-Ito, with some fine perched houses.)

After Ichbakene cross the river to the R bank, and the gorge becomes narrow and high-sided. Throughout this stretch of the river you pass stark, rocky terrain which creates a feeling of other-worldliness. One hour beyond Ichbakene the valley opens out again at an *azib*, Imi n'Ikkis, with a side-valley coming in from the south, which is the approach for the fine cone of Jebel Tizoula, 3447m, the highest point on this southern crest. (The map has it placed further east.) Keep following the river on the R bank and shortly enter an area of willows, then take the path on the L bank.

Ahead the valley broadens considerably to form a large, cultivated basin. There is a prominent isolated kasbah on the R. Now you gain the first decent view of the Mgoun massif – hitherto this has remained hidden. Continue on the L bank of the Tessaout to arrive shortly in the first village, Amezri (2hrs from Ichbakene, 5½hrs from Ait Ali-n-Ito). There is a pleasant campsite on a terrace beneath walnut trees, by the main path just before the village. Alternatively, accommodation in the village should be easy to find. For greater peace, continue to the camp just before Tasgaiwalt.

Day 7 Amezri to Source of Tessaout

This is the day for which you have carried the rope and climbing equipment! Fortunately, as mentioned in the introduction to this section, there is an alternative which goes via a col and doesn't involve any climbing.

If you have the ability to climb a 20m V diff. pitch, with sack if backpacking, then I cannot recommend the Tessaout (Wandras) gorge enough. The rock scenery is some of the most magnificent to be found anywhere, equalling if not surpassing anything in Europe. A canyon with 700m walls, capped in places with huge jutting roofs, and crystal-clear waterfalls combine to make this a tremendous expedition.

The Tessaout gorge, looking downstream from the second 'bad step'

Whichever route you decide to take, both initially continue up the Tessaout valley. From Amezri follow a track through the village along the irrigation channel to reach Tasgaiwalt (40mins). Keep contouring through fields until the river is reached, and follow the R bank (1hr 5mins).

Wade the river at a narrowing between rock walls, just past the concreted start of the irrigation channel. Continue on a track on the L bank to reach a well-defined horizontal track by a large cedar. This is where the two routes divide: for ascending the gorge continue upstream; if taking the easier (though longer) way, turn L along the horizontal track.

Via Tessaout Gorge

Time:	6hrs
Ascent:	700m
Grade:	moderate
Warning:	involves roped climbing; remote location

Continue up the river to where a path joins the river at a small bridge (this is the path from Tessawt-n-Oufella, taken in times of flood, described below).

The river becomes narrow again. The path crosses a crag 15m above the river – straightforward but narrow and airy for a short distance. Continue up the gorge, taking the easiest line on either bank, passing the occasional deserted shelter built into the caves. These are reminiscent of American Indian *pueblos* such as the Canyon de Chelly. These and the hewn cedar logs provide evidence that the Berbers have been here before. Even more remarkable are the little bridges and wooden stairs built across awkward sections. Locals assure me that they take donkeys up here, though the path is too difficult for mules. Keep an eye and ear open for grazing goats, which are apt to knock stones down.

The upper Tessaout gorge

The gorge continues, winding its way in a bewildering series of twists and turns, becoming ever more enclosed and towering. The vegetation here is lush alongside the river. After about 4hrs a 'bad step' of 10m (Moderate in standard) is encountered by a waterfall. This is climbed just L of the waterfall.

Continue past a remarkable little spring emerging from the rock wall to reach an impassable waterfall 30mins further on. Circumventing this is the crux of the whole ascent. From the broad rock platform by the river (just below and out of sight of the waterfall), there is an obvious crack on the R wall of the gorge. It starts from ledges some 10m above the scree and leads to a terrace. Scramble up to the base of the crack and climb it (V diff., 20m, at least two good pegs in place) to the terrace. Be careful of loose rock on the floor of the terrace. Belay pegs are in place.

From here easy scrambling and walking lead past some huge boulder chokes. The gorge starts to lose height rapidly. Continue along it to emerge eventually onto a beautiful upland pasture and campsite. There is a natural rock arch 100m ahead on the right.

Via the Col

Time:	6hrs
Ascent:	900m
Grade:	strenuous

From the junction in the gorge take the horizontal track L and follow a good path north-west past an *azib* (where there is a faint trickle of water only in summer). Begin to bear R, and zigzag up to a prominent gully beneath a series of buttresses. Follow the path almost to the top of the gully, and bear R with it to a col (c.3216m). This is the highest point reached. At the col a faint path bears L across the Tacheddid plateau. (Poor quality water is found 1hr beyond the col.) Wander in and out of a broken crag system for a further 1½hrs. Bear R downhill on a good path towards the top of the gorge. The meadow campsite is visible ahead.

If the river is in spate

From Amezri take the track which leads across the head of the main valley floor towards the RH branch of the upper valley. A good mule track leads around the hill between the two branches, via Tichki and Tassawt-n-Oufella. The path heads north, then north-east at a fork, to descent to

The idyllic campsite at the head of the Tessaout gorge, from where ascents of Irhil Mgoun are made. Note the natural rock arch.

the Jessaout again at the small bridge mentioned. Cross this, and proceed as for the route via the col. Be aware of the risk of flash floods in summer.

Day 8 The Ascent of Mgoun

This route takes you to the highest point in this part of the Atlas, and the only 4000m peak outside the Toubkal region. The actual summit is Amsod (4068m) which is only one part of a long ridge that stretches for several miles at around 4000m. The ascent is straightforward with no technical difficulty, but it is long, and the altitude can be felt by some.

From the campsite follow the main valley north-east to where it opens into a wide plain (20mins). Trend R towards a distant summit on the flat side-valley. Aim towards a 'block-house'-shaped solitary rock straight ahead on the crest of a nearby hill (east). Follow this into the valley, to the base of a spur descending from the main ridge. Skirt the base of the mountain (east-north-east) to the valley. Zigzag up (50mins), continue to a large spur, cross this into a gully and find a prominent track. Continue in the same direction towards a very obvious col and well-defined track – the Tizi-n-Oumsoud (3hrs).

The long scree ascent to the summit ridge of Irhil Mgoun

Looking along the summit ridge to Irhil Mgoun

At the col skirt L on the south side and head up the scree (tiring) to reach the main ridge. Follow this to Pt.3967 (4½hrs), a rocky top. There are permanent snow patches here and frost striations, an indication of conditions in winter. Sacks can be left here, as you return this way. It is still a long way to the summit, though. Continue along a delightful ridge, with superb views if no haze, to Pt.4011 (5¼hrs) and on to the summit (4068m, 6hrs from camp). Note the fossil seashells on the final slope!

To descend, return along the ridge to Pt.3967 (1¼hrs from the summit), then continue down the scree, facing back towards the main summit initially, and skirt L under Pt.3967 to drop to a rocky depression which leads into a deep, broad, stony valley. Descend steeply into this valley, which runs north-north-west to the Tessaout, and head back to the campsite (2½hrs from Pt.3967; 9½hrs–10hrs for the whole trip).

Day 9 Via Tacheddid Ridge to Iskattafene

Time:	8½–9hrs
Ascent:	400m
Grade:	strenuous

The final day's walking offers excellent views and the first opportunity to see the general course of the previous week's walking.

From the campsite follow the shrinking Tessaout to its springs on green meadows. There is a derelict refuge on the left; from it ascend a zigzag path which trends towards the east end of the Tarkeddid ridge. Reach the crest (2hrs 10mins), with a good viewpoint 100m to the R along the ridge. From the crest follow an obvious track, first north-west towards Jebel Tifdaniwine, the prominent pyramidal peak, then down to an *azib*. From the col to Ighil-n-Ikkis head east down a steep valley, passing a welcome spring half-way down.

Jebel Tifdaniwine (3449m) is an obvious possibility, if feeling fit. Traverse the hillside to the L to gain the ridge at the saddle connecting Tifdaniwine to the main Tacheddid ridge. Follow this directly to the summit. To descend, either retrace your steps to the main ridge or drop down from the saddle directly to the *azib*.

Continue down the Arous valley to Ait Said (4hrs), then just before Arous fork R to the main Ait Bougoumez valley. Head R into the valley crossing a plain to arrive at the tarmac road at Igouti, where there are *gîtes* (6–6½hrs). It is still another 2½hrs along the tarmac to Iskattafene; it is longer, but more pleasant, through the fields.

Variation

Time:	8hrs
Ascent:	200m
Grade:	moderate
Warning:	involves abseil

An interesting gorge variation is possible, involving an abseil. From the Tessaout sources continue east over the watershed to descend to the Arous drainage. Follow the stream-bed into the gorge.

The gorge is very narrow in places, where the river has cut through the severely folded rock. The waterfall is circumvented by an 18m abseil (piton belays). The abseil puts you into the pool at the base of the waterfall! Follow the gorge (springs falling down on left), which is still interesting but easy, to emerge in a broad willow valley. This soon leads to a junction with the normal route.

If you desire to see the gorge and its springs without having to abseil, turn R (upstream) at the Arous after descending from Tacheddid. (There is a good campsite above the river.) The river can be followed as far as the waterfall. Immediately on entering the gorge from below, notice the slender cascade high on the L. This is very beautiful and easily missed when descending. It is possible to scramble easily up to the base of this fall, which is set back from the main gorge.

OTHER EXCURSIONS IN THE MGOUN AREA

The long ridges and escarpments provide ample scope for day and multi-day walks. Unlike the ridges in the Toubkal region these present few technical difficulties. The following list merely gives an indication of the potential; visitors will undoubtedly discover routes of their own.

Mgoun (4068m)

The continuation ridge north-east from the summit provides a magnificent walk, which leads eventually into the Mgoun gorges.

Mgoun can be reached from the south, and this is perhaps one of the easiest ways of ascending the peak. Your own transport is essential, however. From Ouarzazate drive to Skoura, then north to Amekchoud and and on to the roadhead at Aguerd-n'Igherm. From here head north-east straight up the valley to Tighouzzirine, from where a track leads northwards onto the long south spur desending from the summit ridge. Head steeply up to gain a subsidiary ridge, which leads to the main ridge and the summit. Jebel Aklim, 3432m, is worth taking in if possible, and gives a grandstand view of the Mgoun crest.

Tacheddid

This provides another fine ridge scramble. From the campsite beneath Mgoun it is a 6–8hr round trip.

Tessaout Gorge Peaks

The Mgoun crest west of the Tizi-n-Oumsoud goes over Jbel-n-Nig Oumassine (3883m) and Jbel Tazoult-n-Ouguerd (3877m), big rolling hills worth traversing to return along the lip of the Tessaout gorge.

Azurki (3690m)

The very prominent limestone escarpment dominating the view up the Ait Bougoumez valley. From the col on the old road into the valley it provides an enjoyable day's walk, and is a popular ski mountain too.

Jebel Aroudane (Aioui) (3382m)

A continuation of the Azurki ridge eastwards, its northern cliffs offer one of the great rock-climbing areas. These cliffs, together with the spires above Zawyat Ahancal, are often called the Dolomites of the Atlas.

The Mgoun Gorges

Allow three to four days for the full experience of the gorges.

From the Tacheddid plateau head east to descend the Oulilimt valley. There is good camping at the Tighremt-n-Ait Ahmed, where the track from Tabant and the Bougoumez joins, having crossed the Tizi-n-Ait Imi (2905m). Villages lead on to the last, facing Imi Nirkt on the map. This is where the fun starts. There is a day or two of constant wading between soaring cliffs – it is very committing, and the danger of flash floods must be kept in mind. Between Tafelka and Tiranimine there are no camping spots. At one stage a cliff-face traverse ends with a built-up 'ladder' down to the narrowest gorge section. A dirt track can be picked up at Aguerzaka, but continuing to Issoumar is recommended.

JEBEL SAHRO

The Jebel Sahro is a range of mountains between the High Atlas and the Sahara, and is the eastern continuation of the Anti-Atlas. These mountains are separated from the main Atlas range by the Dades and Draa valleys. In contrast to the greener, more fertile slopes to the north,

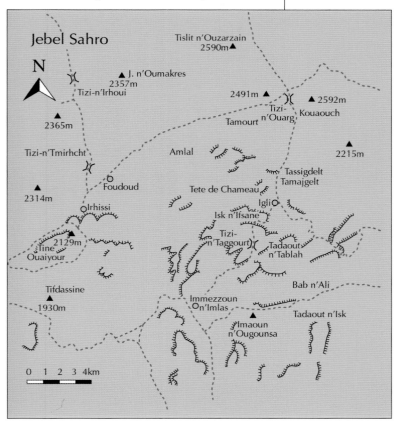

the landscape in these valleys is one of vivid oases set beneath barren mountain slopes. Palm trees abound, and roses form hedgerows between small fields. There are several hundred miles of rose hedges, harvested to produce rose attar, and during the period of flowering they provide a beautiful sight.

Architecturally, the region is stunning, with countless mud-brick kasbahs lining the road. Unfortunately, as in other areas, these are falling into disrepair, but sufficient remain to leave a lasting impression on the visitor. Noteworthy in this respect are Skoura, the huge kasbah at Ouarzazate, nearby Ait Benhaddou, and the lower Dades area. Even if there is no time for walking, it is worth spending a couple of days exploring this area.

The Jebel Sahro mountains are starkly beautiful, and offer a sense of isolation not to be found in the more populated ranges to the north. When I first visited this region in the late 1980s, ours was one of the first commercial groups to trek in the area. Subsequently several tour companies have started to offer treks here. Despite the growth in popularity, the overriding experience is one of solitude and remoteness, affording the discerning traveller a more authentic, less commercialised view of Morocco. Untainted by hordes of trekkers, the inhabitants seem more hospitable and friendly as a result.

The Jebel Sahro is a region of contrasts. One minute a trail may lead beneath date palms or through almond groves watered by an ancient well, the next minute it may cross a stony plateau where nomads in their black felt tents scrape a living. The atmosphere is that of a biblical wilderness, with shepherds playing reed flutes and the occasional camel visible, silhouetted against the skyline. The scenery is often magnificent, with flat-topped mesas and buttes forming a backdrop to deep gorges and tottering pinnacles of conglomerate.

As a whole the area possesses a magic which will appeal to anyone with a sense of adventure. It is not without its problems and hazards: this is wild country, with few roads. The people are unused to visitors, so dealings can take some time.

The best time to visit is from October through to March; outside these months it is likely to be uncomfortably hot. In the winter months, however, do not underestimate the cold. There is a heavy frost on most nights and during the day it can be bitterly cold as well. Snow is usual in January, but normally during this period one can expect to find the sun shining and daytime temperatures in the mid-60s to 70s Fahrenheit. It is essential to bring a good four-season sleeping bag, and preferably a duvet jacket for the long, cold nights.

The central and most dramatic part of the range is focused around the rock pinnacles surrounding the hamlet of Igli. The easternmost of these are known as the Bab'n Ali ('gates of Ali') and can be accessed via a rough four-wheel-drive track (see below). Consequently, it is possible to undertake a relatively short visit here, taking in the best scenery.

The circuit described below is a nine-day tour, which (allowing for time spent purchasing supplies, hiring mules, etc) could easily be done in a two-week holiday from Marrakech or Agadir.

Looking across to the Tete de Chameau from the top of Tassigdelt Tamajgalt

123

ACCESS

Marrakech and Agadir both serve as suitable starting-points. From Marrakech go via the Tizi-n'Tichka to Ouarzazate, then east along the P32 to Kelaa des Mgouna (6hrs driving time). From Agadir go inland as far as Ouarzazate, then join the route from Marrakech as described above.

Buses depart regularly from Marrakech and Agadir for Ouarzazate. Continuing east along the P32 there are plenty of local buses and shared taxis. There is an airport at Ouarzazate, from where there are flights to Europe, a Club Med and various other large hotels.

One of the pleasant surprises for visitors to the south side of the Atlas is the number of good hotels. The area is very popular with the French in winter, and it is possible to sleep and dine in comparative luxury here.

Kelaa des Mgouna is the starting point for the trek described, but the range can also be accessed from Boumalne or Tinerhir – useful if you are also visiting the Todra gorge.

TOWN SUPPLIES

There are several large towns along the Dades valley, which means that the purchase of supplies is relatively easy and it is not really necessary to stock up in Marrakech.

Ouarzazate is the largest and best-stocked town, though furthest from the mountains, and Western foods are best purchased here. Otherwise continue on to Kelaa des Mgouna (Kelaa), where everything needed can be obtained and where there is a large market (reasonably priced). Furthermore Kelaa is much the closest town to the start of the trek. Boumalne, 22km north-east along the valley, is similar though smaller and with much less choice. Further east, Tinerhir is similar to Boumalne in its variety of shops.

Ouarzazate, Kelaa and Boumalne have hospitals and chemists.

Tinerhir has a recommended campsite, the Camping Atlas, at around 16dh per night.

SUPPLIES EN ROUTE

It would be hard to eat well on food purchased en route. Bits and pieces are available, but don't rely on these when stocking up. It is best to regard them as variety, rather than as staples.

Eggs and dried dates can be found in most villages, and in more unlikely places too; sometimes a small girl will run over from her flock of sheep and hold out a handful of eggs. In the villages chickens are not expensive, and delicious bread can often be found. Elsewhere a sheep or goat can always be purchased, and the muleteers will happily prepare it over an open fire. Occasionally almonds are available, but these are an important cash crop and are not sold cheaply.

Gas refills are not available anywhere, so be sure to take sufficient with you. For lighting fires there is an abundance of dry brush, which flares up quickly. This is inefficient for cooking, but it is what the locals use.

Finally, the cleanest supply of water is often in the wells. These may not have buckets attached, so it is worth carrying some string for lowering water bottles.

Craft workers enjoying the winter sun, Dades valley

BASES

Ait Youl

The circuit described starts and finishes in the village of Ait Youl, south of Kelaa des Mgouna, on the edge of the barren valley plain. From the main street turn R just after the market (when heading towards Boumalne), then head along a stony track for 4km to the north bank of the Dades river. Cross via a footbridge into the village. The local mosque and its minaret form a prominent landmark on the southern fringes of the village.

It is possible to hire mules and local guides here. The houses will take in visitors for a small charge (try the house on the very edge of the village, about 250m south-east of the minaret). If you arrive late in the evening spend the night in Kelaa, accommodation is hard to find in Ait Youl after everyone has locked and bolted the entrance to their courtyard.

Iknion

Iknion, 40km south-east of Boumalne, is the best base for exploring the eastern section of the Jebel Sahro, including Jebel Fengour and Amalou n'Mansour. Several trekking groups use Iknion as a base. This has the advantage of familiarising the locals with trekkers' needs, but it can be a disadvantage if a group is in the area, as there will be fewer mules available for hire.

Nkob

Often groups trek from Nkob on the south-east flanks of the range. Smaller than Iknion it has fewer facilities, but mules can be hired here. Access to the main eastern part of the range is fairly easy from here.

Approach via Bab n'Ali

At the time of writing (2003) this approach unsuitable for all except four-wheel-drive vehicles, but as this is a popular form of transport for visitors I include a description here. A very rough dirt track runs from Tinerhir to Nkob via the Tizi-n'Tazazert and Bab n'Ali.

The road improves slightly from Bab n'Ali to Nkob. Unsuitable for *grands taxis*, large trucks do ply this route, so it may be possible to get a lift by asking around in Tinerhir or Nkob. There is a cafe (very basic) at the summit of the Tizi-n'Tazazert, and a couple of small campsites, which are equally basic, at Bab n'Ali. These cost 10dh per night, and have hot showers (!) and sell soft drinks. From Bab n'Ali, there is a view towards the pinnacles of Tassigdelt Tamajgalt and the other towers surrounding Igli; the approach is obvious and close by.

A CIRCUIT OF THE REGION

Day 1 Ait Youl to El Mersse Puit

Time:	6½hrs
Ascent:	300m
Grade:	moderate

This first day's walking is rather tedious as it involves crossing the wide, stony expanse between the Dades river and the mountains proper. However, as it is the first day on trek, any boredom will be alleviated by the novelty of the experience.

From the new minaret in Ait Youl head south-east towards an obvious low valley across the stony plain. Trend R to reach a small cultivated area on the banks of a wadi (20mins), where there is a prominent long, low house above the trees. Pass the house on its R (south) side via a decent mule track, heading south-south-east, leaving the valley.

Some 300m beyond the house enter a tiny dry valley. Follow the L bank for another 200–300m or so and emerge onto a low plateau spur. The path continues across this spur to descend into a larger valley. Cross this diagonally (45mins) and keep heading south. The nearby hill to the south-east is Afoughal (2196m). Its eastern flanks are skirted on the return route.

Continue roughly south, skirting a basin on the L. Cross a little ridge (1hr) to enter another broad valley. Follow the track on the L. After 10mins of this the path turns R (still going south) and crosses the valley floor. A further 5mins leads to the main wadi bed (1¼hrs). Walk along this (usually some water in winter), passing a concrete well and drinking trough whose water is filthy and stagnant (1hr 25mins). A few hundred metres beyond the well the riverbed bends to the L – keep straight on south-east. Pass a small stone enclosure 50m further on, on the L. Trend R to continue southwards (1hr 35mins) and join a motorable track.

All the previous section is vague and indistinct on the ground; route-finding becomes much easier as the day progresses.

After 2hrs or so the path branches R off the main track, heading straight towards the distant highest peak on the southern skyline. It leads down into another big valley, with a prominent black rock island in its bed. There is a small settlement below this, and the track leads to the L of the houses in about 2hrs 40mins. The good track continues along the valley, passing a fourth *pise* house and courtyard; the low, square plan contrasts strongly with the previous house's rectangular *ksar* arrangement and tower in the centre north wall. Continue past a small house with a large tree that is very distinctive. There is a well here with good water but no bucket.

The path trends R (south) here and forsakes the main valley for a little valley on the R. Continue towards Afoughal and a house on its northern flank. Just before this is a stream and a tiny rocky gorge. Skirt the mountain on the R, heading south. After 4hrs 25mins you reach a good large well on the edge of fields (a fine lunch spot).

Continuing south enter a narrowing valley with a fair amount of thorn vegetation and running water. At a stone 'blockhouse' (5½hrs) the path keeps L (south) below the crags. Ahead is a large basin (and before it a deep ravine), which is delightfully verdant. Cross the ravine, and a further 10mins across the plain see trees on the R. These trees mark the site of the *puit* (well) at El Mersse. There is a good campsite (6½hrs).

Day 2 El Mersse Puit to Assaka-n'Ait Ouzzine

Time:	5–5½hrs
Ascent:	400m
Grade:	moderate

From the well at El Mersse head north-east across the plain to an obvious low point on the skyline. After 200m, however, gain a track heading south-east which leads diagonally across the hillside to a ridge top (35mins). Here there are fantastic views of the Mgoun ridge and along the main Atlas chain as far as Toubkal. To the west Jebel Siroua is prominent in isolation, and the Dades valley unfolds beneath you. Ahead, the landscape is craggier, with low scrub covering the hillsides. The prominent large plateau to the south-east is Keftent (2095m).

The well-defined track continues south to reach the Tizi-n'Tagmout (1754m) in 1½hrs. Drop down into the broad valley, which possesses a few scattered houses and trees. The route now begins to head E towards the central Jebel Sahro. Take the path east-north-east along the broad valley, which is flanked by Amgroud (2259m) to the south. Ahead lies a very prominent flat-topped mesa – Tine Ouaiyour (2129m).

The valley bottom narrows as the path takes the south side above the wadi bed. Assaka-n'Ait Ouzzine comes suddenly into view, with its beautiful old kasbah, and fruit and palm trees (4hrs 40mins). Don't enter the village, but keep on the near bank of the wadi and head south to where it turns west. After a few hundred metres of following the wadi bed (5hrs) turn back south up a low ridge to join another tributary (5hrs 5mins). Walk along this tributary in an easterly direction for 5mins to enter another, smaller village known as part of Assaka-n'Ait

An idyllic pool near Assaka n'Ait Ouzzine

Ouzzine (5hrs 10mins). From its eastern end one can see a very fertile area on the opposite bank with a ruined kasbah. The soft, water-soluble nature of the *pise* walls means that such buildings have only a 20–30 year life once they are abandoned.

Day 3 Assaka-n'Ait Ouzzine to Irhazzoun n'Imlas

Time:	6½hrs
Ascent:	250m
Grade:	moderate

Continue eastwards along the valley, which is wonderfully fertile in comparison with the previous two days. Note the well, complete with old wooden pulley wheel (10mins). After 1hr reach another small village, Tajalajt. There are signs of modernisation here, with diesel-engined water pumps and new houses.

Continue to the next village, Akerkour (1hr 40mins), a small hamlet with a few well-watered fields. The bulbuls here are very vocal in amongst the palms. Keep walking along this valley, which suddenly opens out (3½hrs). The mountain ahead to the east is Tassigdelt Si (Sidi) el Haj (1722m), which has some impressive escarpments.

After 4¾hrs, and heading in a roughly east-north-east direction, you encounter a few houses around a river meander with several fields. All along this stretch of valley the churring of sandgrouse can be heard; they are extremely secretive birds and difficult to spot.

Continuing north-east the scenery becomes ever more arid and assumes an aspect reminiscent of the American southwest: broad scrub plains, with flat-topped mesas and buttes. The path leads beneath a huge cliff on the R (the largest seen so far) to gain a small col. At the col (6hrs) is the first view of the Bab-n'Ali ('gates of Ali'): this is the huge pinnacle in the distance to the east, with the eroded pinnacles of the Tadaout n'Tablah to its L.

Head initialy east then drop down, after 200–300m, into a gully. The prow of the cliff is very impressive from this angle. Continue down to the broad plain and the village of Irhazzoun n'Imlas (6½hrs).

Day 4 Irhazzoun n'Imlas via Taggourt Plateau to Igli

Time:	3½–4hrs
Ascent:	300m
Grade:	moderate

Head initially towards the Bab-n'Ali pinnacle (east), then veer slightly L towards an isolated building. Growing on the borders of the fields here, seemingly abandoned, are tiny round melons. Don't bother tasting them, they are extremely bitter.

Walk along the sandy wadi bed, which contains one or two palm trees and some very brackish water. This soon becomes a gorge and just as soon finishes (30mins). Ahead lies a fine pinnacled rock formation: the Tadaout n'Tablah. Cross the slabs to gain a track above the wadi bed which leads north-north-east out of the wadi. Emerge (45mins) onto the edge of another wadi, with further fantastic organ-pipe rock formations ahead. The path winds its way towards the nearest formations (super views looking back from here). Aim to the L (north) of this formation (the Tadaout n'Tablah) and gain a slight ridge. The view from here is even better, with the narrow rock spine of the Tête de Chameau ('camel's head', Ighf L'Ghoum in Berber) and Tassigdelt Tamajgalt formations appearing for the first time, along with other equally fantastic plugs and spires.

Approaching the spectacular rock towers of the Taggourt plateau

You are now on the Taggourt plateau. Just to the L (2hrs 10mins) is a cliff, over which the stream flows, and a couple of palm trees. On my first visit here I was welcomed by an old man with a plateful of dates. He was living in a black felt tent nearby with a wife, who looked 40 years younger than himself, and their three children. As she was baking on an open fire I waited until the bread was ready and purchased a few loaves. This was life at its most basic; there was nothing super-fluous amongst their few meagre possessions. The woman wore exquisite, heavy silver jewellery and brilliantly patterned clothes, but otherwise there was no ornamentation to their existence.

The route continues across the plateau towards the Tête de Chameau in a north-north-easterly direction. As this is a short day you may wish to explore the Tadaout n'Tablah pinnacles. To do so, instead of continuing across the plateau head north-east to gain the gap between the two LH rock masses. At the gap a gully leads easily up onto the top of the Tadaout n'Tablah plateau. On top there are fine views all around, with nearby towers and the twin plugs of the Bab-n'Ali to the south-east.

Back on the normal route the huge isolated plug on the L has cairns on top (climbed by whom is a mystery). Drop down from the edge of the plateau (the Tizi-n'Taggourt, 2½hrs) into a valley which has one or two fields and a house on top of a ridge. The track weaves through fields and past further houses, heading towards the Tête de Chameau again. At the end of the fields (3hrs 20mins) head steeply up the R bank. This leads in 10–15mins to a further cultivated area and one or two houses in a cirque, hemmed in by cliffs on three sides. This is Igli (3hrs 35mins), a rest spot for the night. The Tête de Chameau (see Day 5) makes a good afternoon excursion from here.

Day 5 Igli
It is worth spending a day in this area to explore the surrounding cliffs. Directly above the campsite to the

The cultivated fields of Igli

north-east is the Tassigdelt Tamajgalt, while to the north-west is the long mesa of the Tête de Chameau. Of the two the Tassigdelt Tamajgalt is the more worthwhile, although both can be done in one day. East-south-east lies the nearby conical point of Isker (2099m), not nearly as interesting as its neighbours.

Tassigdelt Tamajgalt

Tassigdelt Tamajgalt is a large cliff-ringed plateau. On its Sern edge there is an outlier separated by a rift. The top of this outlier can be gained from its eastern flanks by following a system of gullies. It is terrific fun exploring these clefts in the rock: the route I took to the summit passed between the main cliff body and an outlying spire (70–100m) with an ancient pine decorating its summit. The gap is only 1–2m wide, and is spanned by a chockstone. Further crawling under boulders and easy scrambling gains the top. No doubt future visitors will find alternative routes.

This massif, and all the other rock pinnacles in this area, is formed from a soft 'pudding-stone' conglomerate. On the summit of the outlier there is a thin capping band of hard but soluble limestone, down through which the water has cut and eroded the softer 'pudding-stone' below. This has created the very deep fissures which criss-cross this entire outlier and are, for the most part, narrow enough to step or jump over. Some of the larger gullies contain sizeable ash trees. On top, the flat summit is covered in white alyssum. One can only wonder what the vegetation of this region would be like without the ever-present sheep and goats.

On the western side of the block is a pinnacle reminiscent of Yosemite's 'Lost Arrow spire', separated from the main outlier by a 5m gap. Unclimbed as yet, it offers interesting possibilities to climbers who visit this area. Visible from the outlier summit (behind and just R of Isker) is Jebel bou Rhdad (2334m). The low ridge to the R on the near skyline is a large, flat-topped plateau called Jebel Aneffid.

The pinnacles that ring the edge of the Tassigdelt Tamajgalt plateau

Tête de Chameau

When you tire of exploring this wonderland move across to the Tête de Chameau. This is easily reached by aiming for the lowest point of the tower on its LH (southern) edge. Unlike its neighbour, the top here cannot be reached by scrambling, and as far as I am aware has yet to be climbed. Several pairs of Barbary falcons nest here. It is possible to skirt the base of the cliffs right around the tower, with only a short (8m) section of easy scrambling at the northern end.

Day 6 Igli to Tamourt

Time:	4–4½hrs
Ascent:	450m
Grade:	moderate

This is another very good day, with an optional ascent of a rocky peak by the Tizi-n'Ouarg. The route passes initially via the reddish rock intrusion between Tassigdelt Tamajgalt cliffs. The path leads above the gully bottom, up through rock slabs, and through ground rich with grazed palm fronds and bushes. It then moves well to the R, out of the gully bed, and traverses horizontally. Barbary ground squirrels are common here, providing good food for the hawks which nest amongst the crags.

Follow this path, which leads to the top in 1hr 40mins and emerges onto a hummocky rock plateau. I recall hearing a shepherd playing a reed pipe in the midst of this desolation. Drop down to a wadi which makes a 90° bend on arrival; the Tizi-n'Ouarg is straight ahead to the north-north-east. (**Note:** At this point the escape route to Tiouit heads E along the little tributary wadi on the R.) Cross the stream and ascend to the L (west) side. A gradual ascent leads into the bowl surrounded by tops collectively known as Kouaouch (2hrs 55mins). Looking back, the north side of Tassigdelt Tamajgalt is revealed as a gentle slope. If time and energy permit, it is worth climbing the little peak to the north: 8–10m of easy scrambling on the S face to gain the summit overlooking the precipitous N face (c.80m). There are outstanding views from here in all directions, from the snow-capped Mgoun ridge to the Tazzarine valley in the south.

Walk on to the Tizi-n'Ouarg (3hrs 20mins) and descend south of west. A distinctive feature on the descent is the 20 or so trees which are scattered on the slope. Drop down between rounded tops and continue in a roughly west-south-west direction. About 45mins from the col you reach a small, flat grassy area by a stream, below the peak of Tamourt. This is a good campsite, though cold due to the altitude (4hrs 5mins).

Day 7 Tamourt to Irhissi

Time:	6½hrs
Ascent:	300m
Grade:	moderate

Continue west-south-west across featureless pasture until the valley starts to pass beneath the large bulk of Jebel Amlal on its south side. The valley becomes flanked by tall cliffs. Follow the stream down as it leads beneath impressive crags. Half-way down the valley there are a few small shelters belonging to the semi-nomadic herders who scratch a living here. About 10mins beyond the houses there is another small shelter on the R. Just before this on the LH side are several graves. Graves in these parts are simple affairs, being a low pile of stones with a solitary, uninscribed headstone. Once recognised, many similar burial areas close to paths and habitation become apparent.

At the bottom of this valley to the south-west you reach a small settlement – Foudoud. The track winds behind it then climbs steeply up and over the ridge. Descend from the ridge into a small valley and follow it down, through increasingly impressive scenery, to arrive at a ruined kasbah at the confluence of two valleys. This is Irhissi (6½hrs), which makes a fine camping place.

Day 8 Irhissi via Assaka n'Ait Ouzzine to Tafoughalt

Time:	7½–8hrs
Ascent:	500m
Grade:	strenuous

This is another fairly long day with a steep ascent after lunch. Rather than continuing in a south-west direction, it is more interesting to skirt the flat-topped bulk of Tine Ouaiyour (2129m) via its southern side.

From the field near the kasbah, cross the stream to its south bank and enter the narrow gorge (Gorge du Irhissi), which heads south almost immediately. Follow the zigzag track pleasantly up through the gorge to emerge after 25mins opposite small conglomerate cliffs.

Approaching the spectacular cliffs of Tine Ouayour

Tine Ouaiyour is very close now. Gain the top of the gentle spur after 50mins. There is another simple graveyard by the track here. There is a fine view east towards Tassigdelt Tamajgalt, and on the R skyline in the far distance is Jebel Bou Gaffer. The near mountain north of east is Jebel Amlal.

The track leads round Tine Ouaiyour to the south-west flank. After 1hr 20mins you skirt a gully – don't take the path on its L (opposite) bank. After 6–7mins your path starts to descend gently south-west to the valley. Cross the undulating plain, and after about 2hrs 40mins see on the L the deep valley taken on the morning of Day 3. The path keeps high on the L bank. After 4hrs 5mins Assaka-n'Ait Ouzzine comes into view – one is better able to appreciate the architecture from this viewpoint than from the other side of the valley.

Continue through Assaka-n'Ait Ouzzine, passing between a kasbah on the L and a *ksar* on the R (noticing the difference in styles). Head R up through the village and continue north across rock slabs to gain a faint path. Cross the ridge (4hrs 20mins) and descend to a solitary palm tree. The route then winds up the hillside towards big crags and no apparent exit.

Pass the RH toe of a large crag (5½hrs), continue up the gully and finally emerge on easier-angled ground (5¾hrs). The summit of Tine Ouaiyour is now well below you, but the top of the pass is still another 35mins away. This affords stunning views both north and south. To the north the Mgoun ridge is prominent, L of this is Annrhomar and to the R the prominent split in the range marks the Gorge du Dades. Further west Meltsene and the Toubkal massif are visible, while below stretches the Dades valley.

Descend east paralleling the ridge and walk along a spur to the north-east (5mins from the top; 6hrs 25mins). Drop down to the L. This leads in the general direction of Afoughal to the north-north-west, and down to a solitary house and fields in a flat basin surrounded by low granitic-looking rock outcrops. This is Tafoughalt (7hrs 35mins).

Day 9 Tafoughalt to Ait Youl

Time:	4½–5hrs
Ascent:	300m
Grade:	moderate

About 100m west of the house head R (north) across a low rocky rise, past a prominent large, upright boulder. West of north is a gap on the skyline through low bouldery ridges. The path weaves its way here (10mins). A sudden view of the Dades valley makes you realise the height of the previous night's campsite.

Drop down the valley, passing Afoughal on the L. After 1hr 5mins pass houses by the path on the L above. About 5mins further on there is a gully, either side of which are caves inhabited seasonally by nomads. It is common to see nomads on this route, as an agreement exists between those of the Ait Bougoumez region and

The main Atlas range is clearly visible from the Jebel Sahro in winter

those of the Jebel Sahro. In summer the nomads of the Jebel Sahro ascend to the central High Atlas, whose nomads in turn make a winter migration down here.

Cross a spur on the west bank of the main wadi (1¼hrs) and continue in the same direction. After 2hrs 20mins pass more caves on the R, this time for goats. The trail starts to leave the main valley-bed for its east side, heading first north-north-west, then north up a tributary. Head steeply up past some more caves for several hundred metres and, with diversions north-west, gain a col after 2hrs 55mins. Follow the track down to where it joins a motor track after 4hrs 10mins. Leave the motor track almost immediately, keeping on down the valley, until after 15–20mins the path ascends the hill ahead.

At the top you can see down into the Dades valley, but Ait Youl is still invisible. After 4hrs 40mins you emerge onto a ridge which is followed round and leads eventually to the prominent white minaret of Ait Youl and the end of the circuit.

Continuation: Valley Walk to Boumalne

Time:	variable – up to 8hrs
Ascent:	level terrain
Grade:	easy

If time permits, it is possible to walk along the Dades valley from Ait Youl to Boumalne. This provides a contrast to the previous days on trek, with walking through fields and orchards. You will realise why this is known as the Valley of the Roses – every field and irrigation ditch is lined with low rose bushes. These are used in the production of rose water, and it is estimated that there are around 4200km of rose hedges around here. In total the walk is around 22km (14 miles), but can easily be terminated simply by heading north-west to the main P32 road, which is never far away. Shared taxis pass along this road every few minutes.

Apart from the flowers in spring, the main interest lies in the many ruined kasbahs along the route. A decline in the importance of agriculture, together with the inflow of money from overseas workers, has led to valley houses being abandoned for newer houses next to the main road. This, together with the disappearance of the extended family, has resulted in these fabulous buildings being left to rot. It is an eerie experience to wander around these places that seem largely intact, with only a collapsed wall or pile of rubble to remind you that they are slowly crumbling away.

Of particular note is the kasbah of El Gomte, near Imadnaghene. Unlike the other kasbahs passed en route this one is in a good state of preservation. It was built by the government during the 19th century and consists of two large kasbah buildings either side of a courtyard, surrounded by a large, intact fortified wall. The high standard of construction and decoration (such as the green-tiled gateways) mark this as a special building.

ESCAPE ROUTES

In the event of accident or illness there are hospitals in Boumalne and Kelaa des Mgouna. They can be reached within a day from most parts of the trek. In addition there are medical facilities at the small mining town of Tiouit.

From the Eastern Section of the Circuit: Igli–Tiouit

Time:	4½hrs
Ascent:	400m
Grade:	moderate

From Igli follow the route as described on Day 6 to the gap between Tassigdelt Tamajgalt and its western neighbour (1hr 40mins). Continue as for this route as far as the right-angled bend at the wadi (1hr 50mins). Turn R up the little tributary. Follow this in amongst rock outcrops, generally east-north-east, for 400m before the path quits the bed for the R bank. Go over a small rise to regain the wadi bed. These are the northern slopes of Tassigdelt Tamajgalt and are very barren.

About 30mins after leaving the main trail the tributary ends in a cwm, and the track takes the gap in the continuation line (north-east). Drop steeply down into a deep valley, and walk straight across this and up the opposite bank. You are now in a region of quartzite, and the landscape changes noticeably, its steep, shattered crags reminiscent of the Toubkal region. Go up over the rocky crest to overlook a deep branch of the same valley you have just left (1hr; 2hrs 50mins in total).

Walk along the L flank of this valley on a horizontal traverse. The rocky peak on the R is Azlou (2215m).

The Oasis of Igli

143

Fields come into view on the opposite bank after 3hrs and seem out of place in this wild landscape. Descend, and at the furthest field take the RH valley branch (3hrs 5mins). The LH branch leads to the Tizi-n'Irgounene. By two large fig trees and a rock pool (3hrs 20mins) the path starts to climb the R bank. After 3hrs 50mins you emerge onto a broad saddle. About 1km ahead is a very prominent white blockhouse and mast on top of a steep rocky peak (Tadmamt, 2491m). On the R in the distance the Tizi-n'Tazazert road is visible.

Trend generally north-east on a level track to another saddle (4hrs 5mins). The road is now clearly visible. Iknion comes into view in the distance, just to the L of Tadmamt. A magnificent view unfolds with the High Atlas to the north, and the long crest of Jebel Fengour (2552m) and Amalou n'Mansour (2712m) to the east above Iknion. A further 5–10mins brings mine workings into view – a very incongruous sight. Continue down the dirt road until Tiouit is revealed nestling in its bowl.

This gold- and copper-mining town of 400 workers has an infirmary, telephone and shop. If more comprehensive medical facilities are required continue to Boumalne, 2hrs by Land Rover down a dirt road. The staff at the mine are very helpful. In the past I have been given coffee and almonds in the manager's house while a driver was found to take me down to Boumalne.

From the Central Part of the Circuit: Irhissi via Tizi-n'Tmirhcht to Dades Valley

Time:	6–8hrs
Ascent:	600m
Grade:	strenuous
Warning:	remote in parts

This is a long day's walk, but by walking briskly it can be accomplished in 6–8hrs. Until the Dades river plain is reached the route heads roughly north the whole way.

From the ruins at Irhissi head north up the valley for 25mins until a zigzag track is reached. Follow this, tortuously, on a good track to gain the summit col of the Tizi-n'Tmirhcht. Ahead the route is obvious – it takes the deep valley to where it intersects with a bigger east–west valley, then heads straight up the other side to a further prominent col (the Tizi-n'Irhioui). This is not as far as it looks, and the ground between the two cols can be covered in an hour.

From the Tizi-n'Irhioui descend into the valley to where the hills peter out and the route emerges onto the stony plain. The best plan now is to head out in a north-easterly direction to gain the river as quickly as possible. Cross this and go on up to the main P32 road. **Note:** At this point Kelaa des Mgouna is closer than Boumalne.

OTHER AREAS

The following areas deserve a brief outline as places of potential interest to the trekker. They are mainly well off the beaten track, although parts of the eastern High Atlas are popular with French visitors.

Jebel Sirwa (Siroua) 3305m

Time:	2-day round-trip
Ascent:	1900m
Grade:	strenuous
Warning:	remote, with difficult scrambling to gain the summit

An isolated peak on the edge of the Souss, it is an extinct volcano visible from many of the High Atlas peaks in the Toubkal region. From Jebel Toubkal itself, it lies in an approximately south-easterly direction, 50km distant. It is covered on the 1:100,000 Taliwine map (Feuille NH 29-XVII-3, one of the four maps in the Toubkal area package sold by Stanfords). There are also 1:50,000 sheets to Sirwa.

Although Jebel Sirwa lacks the grandeur of the nearby Toubkal area, it benefits from impressive approach scenery – jagged peaklets, gorges, astonishing rock features and attractive villages.

The best approach is to start from Taliwine, a village on the P32 road, which runs along the south side of the Atlas. Daily buses run each morning from the Bab Doukkala bus station in Marrakech. They take most of the day and cost about 70dh. From Taliwine, where there is a range of accommodation, restaurants and shops, continue via minibus to the village of Akhfamane, 12km or so further east, or Mazwad, a further 9km east along a dirt road, and the point at which trekking proper starts.

From here it is a two-day walk, following the valley through some beautiful villages to gain the summit. Allow three days in total. Ahmed of the delightful Auberge Souktana in Taliwine can organise treks/ascents throughout the region.

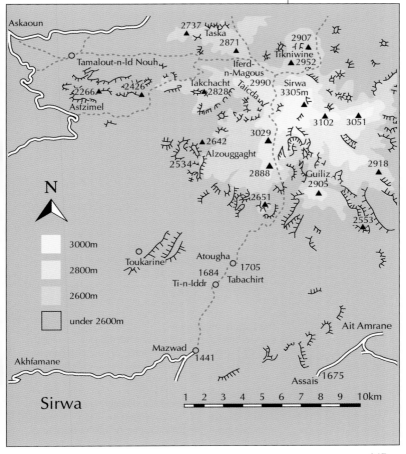

Sirwa

Those with four-wheel-drive vehicles can make interesting approaches to Sirwa from the east or north using the dirt track that encircles the range on its northern side. This is a motoring circuit of great character, with stunning views and great camp sites in green nooks.

Sirwa's summit is a large rocky cone which gives exposed scrambling and some route-finding problems.

The Western High Atlas

The heart of the Western Atlas is the Tichka plateau, a 'lost world' rimmed by peaks with huge cliffs, and offering challenging approaches. Pick-ups run up to the southern villages, from where paths access the Tichka. From the north (via Imi-n-Tanoute or Timesgediouine) there is only one access pass, the Tizi Asdim. The north offers climbing peaks in Ras Moulay Ali (3349m) and Jbel Ikkis (3183m), while to the west runs a crest to Jbel Awlim (3482m) and Tinergwet (3551m), fangs seen well from Taroudant, the usual start (if flying to Agadir). The Oued Nfis drains the Tichka, dominated by Oumzra (5451m), while Igdat (3616m), the highest peak of the Toubkal area, is reached by the Ougdemt valley, off the Tizi-n'Test road. Amizmiz gives access to Erdouz (3579m) and stupendous passes southwards. Barren, unless watered, the area is one of the best in the Atlas. El Aoud Ali, based in Taroudant, has led parties here (and Tichka to Toubkal, a classic trek) for 20 years and speaks English (tel. 06 66 37 972 (mobile)).

The Eastern High Atlas

The most popular base for exploring the area is Imilchil, with its shops, restaurants, mules for hire and autumn festival. Just north of Imilchil is the beautiful Plateau des Lacs, which provides fine walking.

Jebel Ayyashi (3747m) is the most sought-after peak. It is best approached from the north, starting at the small village of Ayt Ouchen, situated on a dirt road between Midelt and Tizi-n'Zou, a few kilometres east of the latter.

The nearest large cities are Beni Mellal, Khenifra, Meknes and Fez; the region's proximity to the prosperous north of the country accounts for its popularity.

The Middle Atlas
The Jbel bon Iblane massif (highest peak Jbel Bou Naceur, 3340m) offers a relatively quiet area, being somewhat remote and best approached from the north-west (Fes). Between this area and the High Atlas are vast cedar forests, a unique landscape to explore.

The Todra and Dades Gorges
Both of these gorges lie on the southern flanks of the main High Atlas and are within easy reach of Boumalne and Tinerhir. While not strictly walking country, they are spectacular and well worth a visit.

The Todra Gorge
This is situated just north of Tinerhir, some 80km east of Boumalne on the P32. A good road leads into the gorge proper where there is a natural spring – the river emerges beside the Yasmina Hotel. At this point bulging cliffs (250m) of solid limestone tower above the gravel base of the canyon. Over the last couple of decades, climbers have started to turn the immense potential for new routes – masses of jamming cracks up steep walls and pocketed limestone faces – into a significant sport climbing area. The winter climate, also, is enviable. There are several hotels at the gorge entrance and two right under the cliffs, including the Yasmina, so accommodation of all standards is easy to find. Tour buses mob the place, but then depart, so staying on is pleasant.

Above the Yasmina a four-wheel-drive vehicle is needed. From the top end of the gorge it is possible to drive in 4–5hrs, across awful roads, to Msemrir and the upper section of the Dades gorges. The current idyllic feel to the area may not last, as a metalled road is being constructed through the gorge. No doubt this will lead to a substantial increase in coach parties visiting the gorge, but the sur-rounding hillsides should still offer escape for the walker.

The Todra gorge

Other accommodation possibilities exist in Tinerhir, including a campsite (see introduction to Jebel Sahro section).

The Dades Gorges

These are situated north of Boumalne. Less visited than the Todra gorge they can be viewed from a tarmac road up to Msemrir. There is much more water flowing in this river and it has several good swimming-holes. Notable features are the 'Bodies Rocks' (pinnacles – worth exploring on foot), side-gorges (ask at the Gazelle inn below the hairpins – a good walking area), and the deeply twisting gorges before Msemrir. Dirt tracks continue to Imilchil or to the top of the Todra (very rough).

APPENDIX 1:
Other Possibilities

The Grand Traverse of the Atlas

This route, devised by Michel Peyron (see Bibliography), stretches from the Western High Atlas to Taza in the north-east. The complete traverse would be a major undertaking of 5–6 weeks' duration, providing an extremely varied and enjoyable traverse. It can be done over several visits, and there are endless options offered, so trekkers can make the route moderate or more challenging as desired. In 1995 a full traverse was made from Taza to Tamri (on the coast) – this took 112 days, covered 900 miles and included the ascent of 30 peaks.

Ski-touring Possibilities

In wintertime the whole of the Atlas provides almost unlimited scope for ski-touring and is already popular with the Swiss and French. January can often have bad weather, while February is usually more settled. Good snow conditions can remain through to March and even April, although spring comes early to the Atlas, and warm sun can produce unpleasantly mushy conditions in the afternoons.

By and large the High Atlas are not very good for *Langlauf*. The area lends itself to ski-mountaineering but cannot really be recommended to the beginner. Full ski-mountaineering kit, including skins, mountaineering bindings and *Harscheissen,* are essential. No doubt the heavier Telemark gear which has been in vogue in recent years will also be useful. On Toubkal the combined South cwm / North cwm circuit is popular, as are ascents of Ouanoukrim summits. In a good year it is possible to ski right down to Sidi Chamarouch. From Tacheddirt the classic tour is to the Tizi Likemt.

There is a French guidebook to the area (*Ski Randonnees dans le Haut Atlas Marocain*) obtainable from the CAF refuge in Oukaimeden, the only real ski resort, and a good place to warm up before any ski-mountaineering. A multi-day Haute Route is of high calibre.

In the central High Atlas the Mgoun area has some excellent possibilities, including that of Mgoun itself. Waougoulzat and Azurki are classic objectives.

The eastern Middle Atlas south of Fes and Taza offers ski-touring in the Bou Iblane area. Snow conditions here are often much better than those encountered further west. There is a very attractive old refuge at Taffert (permanently wardened), which acts as a good base for tours.

Note: It should be added that over the last decade there have been almost snowless winters in the Atlas, with little skiing of note – a worrying trend.

APPENDIX 2:
Bibliography

Clark, B., *Berber Village* (London 1959)
A detailed study of the way of life in a High Atlas community.

Knight, Richard, *Trekking in the Moroccan Atlas* (Trailblazer 2001)
Some treks in the popular areas and also much on Marrakech.

Landau, Rom, *The Kasbahs of Southern Morocco* (Faber & Faber 1969)
A good account of the local architecture; otherwise of little interest.

Peyron, M., *Great Atlas Traverse*. Vol. 1. *Moussa Gorges to Ayt Bou Wgemmaz*. Vol. 2. *Ayt Bou Wgemmaz to Midelt* (West Col 1990)
Gives a linear traverse line the length of the Atlas, with many variants, peaks to climb and knowledgeable background information.

Maxwell, Gavin, *Lords of the Atlas* (Longmans, 1966; republished 2000, illustrated)
A classic account of the rise and fall of the Glaoui tribe, it gives a good insight into life in the region during the period preceding the French protectorate.

Peterson, R.T., Mountfort, G. & Hollom, P.A.D., *A Field Guide to the Birds of Britain and Europe* (Collins 1974)

Hollom, P.A.D., Porter, R., Christensen, S. & Willis, I., *The Birds of the Middle East and North Africa* (Poyser 1988)
Designed to be used in conjunction with the previous book, together they describe every species of bird found in the region.

Dresch, J. & Lépiney, J. de, *Le Massif du Toubkal* (1942)
The book's maps, diagrams, etc, are still very useful.

Bidwell, M. & R., eds., *Morocco: The Travellers' Companion* (I. B. Tauris 1992)
An anthology of Moroccan writing through the centuries.

Hargraves, O., *Culture Shock! Morocco* (Graphic Arts Center Publishing 2001)
An entertaining guide to customs and etiquette.

Of the general guides to Morocco, the following are recommended: The Rough Guide, Cadogan Guide, Footprint Guide, Everyman Guide.

Stanfords (www.stanfords.co.uk) always has a good stock of books and guides, while Atlas Maps (tel. 01592 873546) holds all mountain guides on the Atlas in English and French.

APPENDIX 3:
Glossary

Below is a list of words, both Arabic and Berber, that visitors are most likely to encounter in speech or as map features. Arabic nouns are usually preceded by 'Al' when written – this is equivalent to the word 'the'. On maps, 'Ou', especially at the start of a word, is a **w** sound, eg. Warzazat (Ouarzazate) and final 'e' is not pronounced.

Adrar (Ber.)	mountain
Aguelman (Ber.)	lake
Ain (Ar.) *pl.* Aioun	spring
Ait (Ar.)	tribe (sons of)
Assif (Ber.)	river
Azib (Ber.)	summer hut
Bab (Ar.)	gateway, mouth
Hammam (Ar.)	steam-bath
Imi (Ber.)	gateway, mouth
Irhil (Ar.)	mountain massif
Jebel (Ar)	mountain
Kasbah (Ar.)	fortified house, or village
Ksar (Ar.) *pl.* Ksour	castle, walled stronghold
Marabout (Ar.)	shrine
Oued (Ar.)	river or valley
Sidi, seti (Ar.)	saint
Tizi (Ber.)	col, pass

APPENDIX 4:
Arabic Numbers

1	Waha	2	Juje	3	Tlett'a	4	Rab'a
5	Qhamsa	6	Seta	7	Seb'a	8	Temenya
9	Tis-aa	10	Ash'ra	11	Qad'ash	12	Tn'ash
13	Tlett'ash	14	Rab'atash	15	Qhamst'ash	16	St'ash
17	Sebat'ash	18	Tement'ash	19	Tisat'ash	20	Ash'reen
30	Tletteen	40	Rabaa-een	50	Qhamseen	60	Seteen
70	Seba-een	80	Temenyeen	90	T'saeen	100	Meeya
200	Meetayn						
300	Tletmeeya						
400	Rabaameeya						
1000	Elf						

NOTES

LISTING OF CICERONE GUIDES

IRELAND
The Mountains of Ireland
Irish Coastal Walks
The Irish Coast to Coast

INTERNATIONAL CYCLE GUIDES
The Way of St James – Le Puy to
  Santiago cyclist's guide
The Danube Cycle Way
Cycle Tours in Spain
Cycling the River Loire – The Way
  of St Martin
Cycle Touring in France
Cycling in the French Alps

WALKING AND TREKKING
IN THE ALPS
Grand Tour of Monte Rosa Vol 1
Grand Tour of Monte Rosa Vol 2
Walking in the Alps (all Alpine areas)
100 Hut Walks in the Alps
Chamonix to Zermatt
Tour of Mont Blanc
Alpine Ski Mountaineering
  Vol 1 Western Alps
Alpine Ski Mountaineering
  Vol 2 Eastern Alps
Snowshoeing: Techniques and Routes
  in the Western Alps
Alpine Points of View
Tour of the Matterhorn

FRANCE, BELGIUM AND
LUXEMBOURG
The Tour of the Queyras
Rock Climbs in the Verdon
RLS (Robert Louis Stevenson) Trail
Walks in Volcano Country
French Rock
Walking the French Gorges
Rock Climbs Belgium & Luxembourg
Tour of the Oisans: GR54
Walking in the Tarentaise and
  Beaufortain Alps
The Brittany Coastal Path
Walking in the Haute Savoie, vol. 1
Walking in the Haute Savoie, vol. 2
Tour of the Vanoise
Walking in the Languedoc
GR20 Corsica – The High Level Route
The Ecrins National Park
Walking the French Alps: GR5
Walking in the Cevennes
Vanoise Ski Touring
Walking in Provence
Walking on Corsica
Mont Blanc Walks
Walking in the Cathar region
  of south west France
Walking in the Dordogne
Trekking in the Vosges and Jura
The Cathar Way

PYRENEES AND FRANCE / SPAIN
Rock Climbs in the Pyrenees
Walks & Climbs in the Pyrenees
The GR10 Trail: Through the
  French Pyrenees
The Way of St James –
  Le Puy to the Pyrenees

The Way of St James –
  Pyrenees-Santiago-Finisterre
Through the Spanish Pyrenees GR11
The Pyrenees – World's Mountain
  Range Guide
The Pyrenean Haute Route
The Mountains of Andorra

SPAIN AND PORTUGAL
Picos de Europa – Walks & Climbs
The Mountains of Central Spain
Walking in Mallorca
Costa Blanca Walks Vol 1
Costa Blanca Walks Vol 2
Walking in Madeira
Via de la Plata (Seville To Santiago)
Walking in the Cordillera Cantabrica
Walking in the Canary Islands 1 West
Walking in the Canary Islands 2 East
Walking in the Sierra Nevada
Walking in the Algarve

SWITZERLAND
The Jura: Walking the High Route &
  Ski Traverses
Walking in Ticino, Switzerland
Central Switzerland –
  A Walker's Guide
The Bernese Alps
Walking in the Valais
Alpine Pass Route
Walks in the Engadine, Switzerland
Tour of the Jungfrau Region

GERMANY AND AUSTRIA
Klettersteig Scrambles in
  Northern Limestone Alps
King Ludwig Way
Walking in the Salzkammergut
Walking in the Black Forest
Walking in the Harz Mountains
Germany's Romantic Road
Mountain Walking in Austria
Walking the River Rhine Trail
Trekking in the Stubai Alps
Trekking in the Zillertal Alps

SCANDINAVIA
Walking In Norway
The Pilgrim Road to Nidaros
  (St Olav's Way)

EASTERN EUROPE
Trekking in the Caucasus
The High Tatras
The Mountains of Romania
Walking in Hungary

CROATIA AND SLOVENIA
Walks in the Julian Alps
Walking in Croatia

ITALY
Italian Rock
Walking in the Central Italian Alps
Central Apennines of Italy
Walking in Italy's Gran Paradiso
Long Distance Walks in Italy's Gran
  Paradiso
Walking in Sicily
Shorter Walks in the Dolomites
Treks in the Dolomites

Via Ferratas of the Italian
  Dolomites Vol 1
Via Ferratas of the Italian
  Dolomites Vol 2
Walking in the Dolomites
Walking in Tuscany
Trekking in the Apennines
Through the Italian Alps: the GTA

OTHER MEDITERRANEAN
COUNTRIES
The Mountains of Greece
Climbs & Treks in the Ala Dag
  (Turkey)
The Mountains of Turkey
Treks & Climbs Wadi Rum, Jordan
Jordan – Walks, Treks, Caves etc.
Crete – The White Mountains
Walking in Western Crete
Walking in Malta

AFRICA
Climbing in the Moroccan Anti-Atlas
Trekking in the Atlas Mountains
Kilimanjaro

NORTH AMERICA
The Grand Canyon &
  American South West
Walking in British Columbia
The John Muir Trail

SOUTH AMERICA
Aconcagua

HIMALAYAS – NEPAL, INDIA
Langtang, Gosainkund &
  Helambu: A Trekkers' Guide
Garhwal & Kumaon –
  A Trekkers' Guide
Kangchenjunga – A Trekkers' Guide
Manaslu – A Trekkers' Guide
Everest – A Trekkers' Guide
Annapurna – A Trekker's Guide
Bhutan – A Trekker's Guide

AUSTRALAYS AND NEW ZEALAND
Classic Tramps in New Zealand

TECHNIQUES AND EDUCATION
The Adventure Alternative
Rope Techniques
Snow & Ice Techniques
Mountain Weather
Beyond Adventure
The Hillwalker's Manual
The Book of the Bivvy
Outdoor Photography
The Hillwalker's Guide to
  Mountaineering
Map and Compass

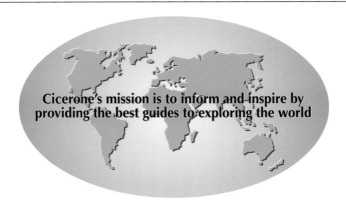

Cicerone's mission is to inform and inspire by providing the best guides to exploring the world

Since its foundation over 30 years ago, Cicerone has specialised in publishing guidebooks and has built a reputation for quality and reliability. It now publishes nearly 300 guides to the major destinations for outdoor enthusiasts, including Europe, UK and the rest of the world.

Written by leading and committed specialists, Cicerone guides are recognised as the most authoritative. They are full of information, maps and illustrations so that the user can plan and complete a successful and safe trip or expedition – be it a long face climb, a walk over Lakeland fells, an alpine traverse, a Himalayan trek or a ramble in the countryside.

With a thorough introduction to assist planning, clear diagrams, maps and colour photographs to illustrate the terrain and route, and accurate and detailed text, Cicerone guides are designed for ease of use and access to the information.

If the facts on the ground change, or there is any aspect of a guide that you think we can improve, we are always delighted to hear from you.

Cicerone Press
2 Police Square Milnthorpe Cumbria LA7 7PY
Tel:01539 562 069   Fax:01539 563 417
e-mail:info@cicerone.co.uk   web:www.cicerone.co.uk

CICERONE